Are We Doing Church Wrong?

REDISCOVERING GOD'S DIVINE
DESIGN FOR HIS CHURCH

Douglas B. Levy

TRILOGY CHRISTIAN PUBLISHERS
TUSTIN, CA

Trilogy Christian Publishers
A Wholly Owned Subsidary of Trinity Broadcasting Network
2442 Michelle Drive
Tustin, CA 92780

For information, address Trilogy Christian Publishing

Rights Department, 2442 Michelle Drive, Tustin, Ca 92780.

Trilogy Christian Publishing/ TBN and colophon are trademarks of Trinity Broadcasting Network.

For information about special discounts for bulk purchases, please contact Trilogy Christian Publishing.

Manufactured in the United States of America

Trilogy Disclaimer: The views and content expressed in this book are those of the author and may not necessarily reflect the views and doctrine of Trilogy Christian Publishing or the Trinity Broadcasting Network.

10 9 8 7 6 5 4 3 2 1

Library of Congress Cataloging-in-Publication Data is available.

ISBN 978-1-63769-438-1

ISBN 978-1-63769-439-8 (ebook)

Contents

Acknowledgements

Jesus, where would I be without You? I don't even want to think about it. Thank You for saving me from myself, giving me purpose, life, fullness, freedom, abundant blessings, and everything else I didn't deserve.

Speaking of things that I didn't deserve: Monica. You have loved me through thick and thin and have stuck with me when I was at my worst. You are such an inspiration to me and are also my favorite human. Thank you for pushing me to be a better me and not giving up on me. Your strengths are definitely a help to my areas of weakness. God couldn't have picked a better woman for me. Thanks for modeling tenacity and finishing so I wouldn't be a quitter. You're the one. Love you, Boo.

Rick Sizemore (& Paula). I love how things have come full circle after almost thirty years. The greatest compliment I could ever pay you will be you seeing line after line, page after page of things you taught me as you read this book. Thank you for fathering me well and opening my eyes to the Scriptures and life with

Jesus in a way that has radically transformed my life. Thank you for ministering into our marriage the way you both did. We would have never made it to twenty-eight years without you two. I can't wait to see what's next as we do family, life, ministry, and kingdom in the present and future.

Bill Goode, my very first spiritual father. Thank you for making sure my feet were planted on the Solid Rock. You and your Tuesday Night Group were the lifeblood for me (and many others) for the first few years of my walk. We were immature, crazy, impossible at times and often didn't know what we were talking about... but you loved us, put up with us, trained us, helped us, prayed for us, and made sure that we didn't fall away or fall into anything stupid. Your crown will be a hundred feet tall with too many jewels and gems to count. I can't wait to see the ripple effect of your life in heaven. I love you and am so thankful that God brought you into my and my family's life.

My family, especially Mom & Dad. Thank you for letting me be "me." You may not have understood some of my life choices initially after becoming a Christian or even agreed with them, but you came around to the call of God on my life. Thanks for the values and life lessons you instilled in me and the love, prayers, and support you've given me. My stepmom Shirley and my mother-in-law Josie: thank you for praying me into the kingdom and loving me like your own. My brother-in-law John: thanks for the use of your "writer's cabin." It was instrumental in me being able to focus and finish this book, and of course, it's a beautiful place to sequester.

To all the churches and many ministry colleagues (way too many to list) that I have been privileged to work alongside with in the kingdom: thank you for encouraging me, inspiring me, sharpening me, ministering to me, loving me, forgiving me, overlooking my weaknesses, flaws, and failures, and letting me discover who I am in Jesus and use my gifts. Thanks to my family, friends, and ministry peers for the valuable feedback.

Introduction:
A Divine Reset

The Lord started giving me the material for this book many years ago, and eventually, I started teaching it, preaching it, and eventually turned it into a Bible study series. When that was happening, the church in America was doing what it had been for decades and maybe even centuries. I have been hopeful that this book would help Christians and churches look again to the authority of God's Word and His design as it related to *the church*. I know it's a long shot, and I've been hopeful that others with more influence than I would join my voice in calling for change.

Then 2020 happened. Specifically, COVID-19 hit, and our collective worlds got turned upside down. Churches stopped meeting in person, were even banned from singing in some places, most churches had to move to an online presence, and suddenly...the church in America didn't look the same. The spiritual landscape of our nation is now completely different.

Right before the pandemic hit and the lockdowns started, my wife and I had gone on a trip to celebrate our anniversary. One day, she asked me what I heard the Lord speaking for this coming year (2020 at the time), and I very clearly heard from the Lord the word "reset."

Now I know that many in the church and ministry world have associated that word with the "great reset" that the "world" is calling for. I believe what the Lord spoke to me in relation to "reset" over the last many months has to do with the church. When God is doing something, usually the world or the enemy launches a counterfeit.

We are at an important moment in church history. I've had conversations with many pastors, leaders, and Christians over the last year. Is this the "new normal?" What will "church" look like, and how will it operate in the coming months and years?

This pandemic has thrust change upon us. Some of it has been good, some of it bad, some of it is yet to be determined. But we've been forced to do things differently, maybe at some churches for the *first time in decades or centuries!*

The church has had to adapt, be creative, take inventory, reprioritize, re-strategize, and figure out what it's supposed to be and for who. Some have made changes. Some are still looking for answers. Some are waiting for things to go back to "normal." But what if there is no "going back?"

Remember Israel and the Exodus? Faced with immense challenges in the wilderness, they were thinking about "going back" (Numbers 11). Lot's wife, too, wanted to "go back." The apostle Paul encourages us with the opposite perspective:

> Brethren, I do not regard myself as having laid hold of it yet; but one thing I do: forgetting what lies behind and reaching forward to what lies ahead, I press on toward the goal for the prize of the upward call of God in Christ Jesus.
>
> Philippians 3:13, 14

The proverbial lightbulb has gone on for a few, and some of my closest ministry friends and associates have realized that their church needs to look different, be different than the way they used to do it. For some, it's big changes, and for others, it's many smaller ones.

My biggest fear is that if down the road there is an opportunity for churches to go back to "church as usual" (read: what they were doing before the pandemic), they will attempt to do it.

There can be comfort in routine, but we already have a Comforter (2 Corinthians 1:3, 4; John 14:16). I believe God wants us to seek *Him* for comfort in the midst of our current craziness and not our routines. He wants to get our churches and us out of our proverbial and literal "comfort zones."

In "Violation of Divine Design," I dig a little deeper in relation to "change" and how God uses it in our lives and how He desires to use it in the church.

I truly believe with all of my heart that God desires a shift within the church. A reset, if you will, not back to church as usual, but back to church according to His Word and His design.

I thank you for taking the time to read this book and prayerfully consider the challenging ideas and scriptures that await you on the following pages.

The Proverbs 24:27 Revelation

I grew up in the Bible Belt, in church. Except for the rare exceptions in my community, it was what you did on Sunday mornings. But I didn't grow up a Christian. And at the age of thirteen, I jumped head first into the ways of the world.

At the age of seventeen, after four years of hardcore rebellion, God found me and saved me. I became the lead singer of a Christian band, and I pursued God with everything I was.

As a born-again Christian, I remember nights of lying awake in my loft bed with a flashlight, my Bible, and a set of highlighters and colored pens. I would read my Student Study Bible and mark any passages that stood out to me, spoke to me, or that I had questions about.

My favorite book in the Bible at the time was the book of Proverbs: straight and simple verses about wisdom and how to "walk" in life. Easy to understand: the wicked does this...the righteous does that...

One night early on in my Christian walk, while reading through Proverbs, I came across this verse that made no logical sense to me. I was stumped. When I first read this scripture, I honestly had no idea what it was talking about. So, for the longest time, I had it highlighted, underlined with *big* question marks beside it...Every now and again, I'd ask the Lord, "What does this mean?"

"Prepare your work outside, and make it ready for yourself in the field; Afterward, then, build your house" (Proverbs 24:27).

As I said, for a season, this made no logical sense to me. If you were a pioneer and had just settled in an area, as any survivalist or prepper will tell you, you *always* build shelter first! Making your work ready in the fields is not a one-day job...

Now, I've read a lot of different interpretations and commentaries about what this could possibly mean, and I'm sure that given the culture of the day, it was probably more of long-term wisdom that applied to those who had already settled, were thinking about marriage and providing for a family, especially in the context of a Jewish family.

Since those early days as a Christian, I've responded to the calling of full-time ministry in the church, and

I've grown in my knowledge and understanding of God's Word and God's ways, but any illumination of this particular passage still had me perplexed.

One day, as I happened across another scripture, I knew the Lord was about to bring a *big* revelation my way about this specific Proverbs passage that I did not understand.

I happened to be reading 1 Corinthians 3:9: "For we are God's fellow workers; you are God's field, God's building."

I said to myself, "Hmmm, where have I heard 'field' and 'building' in the same context before? Aha! The Proverbs passage that has had me stumped!"

So, I went back and read the Proverbs passage and then went back again to 1 Corinthians, chapter three, and re-read it, this time in context. In the first part of this chapter, Paul is using plants as a type referring to us as individuals and then a building as a type referring to us as the church (the *body* of Christ).

The Holy Spirit began giving me insight, wisdom, and revelation as scriptures were brought to my remembrance about "seeds, plants, and trees," mostly speaking in the context of individuals and "stones" being used in the context of the church.

So, as an individual, I am a "plant" that is growing. (Remember the parable of the wheat and the tares? See Matthew 13:24-30.) The goal is for me to be watered and grow and ultimately produce lots of fruit (both fruit of the Spirit on the inside and fruit of ministry on the outside). In John, chapter fifteen, Jesus says He has appointed us to "bear much fruit and that our fruit would remain" (v. 16). This will only happen when the plant/tree is properly cared for and exposed to that which will cause good growth (Psalm 1:3).

So, then God led me to another passage where He showed me that in addition to being a plant, I'm also a part of a *building*: "you also, as living stones, are being built up as a spiritual house for a holy priesthood, to offer up spiritual sacrifices acceptable to God through Jesus Christ" (1 Peter 2:5).

Here, Peter refers to us as "living stones" that are being built into a "spiritual house." "Spiritual house" is a reference for "temple." This gave me even further clarification and revelation into the Proverbs passage. But now, I needed to know what God was saying in terms of the chronological order He spoke of in the Proverbs passage. Why did He say "make your work in the field ready" *first* and then, *afterward*, "build your house?"

Then the Lord gave me the final scripture that tied this multi-scripture, multi-faceted revelation together: "The house [the Temple], while it was being built, was built of stone prepared at the quarry, and there was neither hammer, nor axe, nor any iron tool heard *in the house* while it was being built" (1 Kings 6:7, emphasis and brackets mine).

So, all the work that needed to be done to build the Temple was being done away from the Temple site. The perfecting/finishing work of stone, wood, etc., was done off-site (*"in the field,"* if you will) and brought to the location of the Temple, and then it was fitted together there.

Putting all of these scriptures together, let me complete the big picture together for you:

You are both God's *field* and God's *building*. You are His plant in the field, and you are a living stone in His building. In Proverbs 24:27, we are told to make our work ready in the field and then afterward, to build our house.

We are to allow the Lord to transform us individually (in the field) so that He may fit us together with the other living stones corporately (in His house/temple).

It Is Better to Give Than to Receive

The Holy Spirit began speaking to me about *why* the order was important.

In our modern church culture, we approach and look at Sunday mornings as a place to come get filled, refreshed, encouraged so that we can go out and "face the challenges of Monday–Saturday" only to come back to "church" the next Sunday and repeat the same pattern...

But what if God's design for church was the *exact opposite* of that? What if God meant for us to be getting filled up on Monday–Saturday so that when we come in together on Sunday morning (or whatever day or night we gather corporately), we have something to give instead of needing to get?

You see...when we gather corporately, God wants to take you as a "living stone" and fit you together with other living stones and build His church (spiritual house/temple) corporately. Many times, we come to our services wanting the pastor/preacher/teacher to break open his toolbox and get to work. "Fix me! Chip off my rough edges. Smooth out my splintery grain."

Monday through Saturday, God wants to work on you *in the field* (individually) and get you ready to be fitted together. God has designed the church, His *body*, in such a way that we are *interdependent* on one another. We cannot mature fully spiritually apart from it.

God has designed the church, His *body*, in such a way that we are interdependent on one another. We cannot mature fully spiritually apart from it.

If Christians were to give an honest assessment of why they go to church, I bet most would be willing to admit that it is mainly to receive, to get something out of the experience. The modern Americanized Christian church culture has trained multiple generations to do this.

We want the worship team or leader to lead us in good worship that moves us and brings us into the presence of God, but how many of us spent a significant amount of time in worship on our own, daily, during the week? Even *before* we arrive at our weekly services?

We want the pastor/preacher to preach a great message that speaks directly to what we are going through and give us all the answers we need for our present circumstances and struggles; but how many of us spent quality time studying the Word (2 Timothy 2:15) during the week (apart from a "daily" devotional) to seek out the answers we need for ourselves and learn to hear His voice apart from a sermon or teaching?

Very often, we come to church to get, instead of to give. We come to church to get from God, instead of to give to Him: "God, I need this...God, I need that...God, do this for me...God, get me out of this situation...God, I need you to speak to me..."

We also come to get from people, instead of to give to them, whether it's the pastor, the worship leader, the head of a certain class or ministry. We want people to encourage us, to speak into our lives, to spoon-feed us the Scriptures.

How many of us are so "full" of God from our time spent in worship, Word, and prayer during the week that we are looking for and ready to *pour into others* at our gatherings?

Now, I will make a disclaimer here: there are times when some don't have anything to give and they need to receive. Whether they are "newborn babes" or wounded and hurting, they may indeed need to be poured into for a season. But this should be the exception and not the rule.

> For though by this time you ought to be teachers, you have need again for someone to teach you the elementary principles of the oracles of God, and you have come to need milk and not solid food. For everyone who partakes only of milk is not accustomed to the word of righteousness, for he is an infant. But solid food is for the mature, who because of practice have their senses trained to discern good and evil.
>
> Hebrews 5:12-14

Mature believers should be givers. Mature believers should be able to teach others. As the church, we should, with regularity, be turning sheep into shepherds.

Yes, the church is supposed to be a hospital, but it's not just to heal up the sick and wounded, just so they can go back into the world and get sick and wounded again and come back to church for treatment. We should also be a medical school where we teach and train "spiritual doctors and nurses" to go into the world to heal the sick and treat the wounded.

Mature believers should be givers. Mature believers should be able to teach others. As the church, we should, with regularity, be turning sheep into shepherds.

I believe when you give, you automatically get in return.

> Give, and it will be given to you. They will pour into your lap a good measure—pressed down, shaken together, and running over. For by your standard of measure it will be measured to you in return.
>
> Luke 6:38

"The generous man will be prosperous, and he who waters will himself be watered" (Proverbs 11:25).

The revelation I received from the Lord with these scriptures radically changed my viewpoint of church and understanding a few of the main purposes for us coming together as His church: to be a giver, to cultivate my field during the week, and to be fitted together with the other living stones into the "spiritual house" (temple) that God is building.

Not only did God want to grow me individually during the week, He desires to grow His church when we gather together, but it will require us looking at the church with a new lens and approaching "church" differently than we have up to this point in our current culture.

This revelation was the beginning of many revelations to come from God, helping me see church the way He designed it.

What is the Church?

What are your earliest memories of "church?" Maybe you were very young and have foggy memories of it. Maybe you became a Christian later in life, and church was not something you were exposed to at an early age. You may have very vivid memories, or you may not remember much at all. Maybe your memories were great, or maybe you had bad experiences at church. *Take a moment to reflect on your past church experiences.*

I grew up in a mid-sized United Methodist Church in Southwest Virginia. I have some early memories of pre-school there as a toddler, but that was during the week, not on Sundays. My earliest memories from Sundays are probably of my mom scratching my back during the sermon of our liturgical service when I was around four years old.

I remember playing Dots and Boxes with my sister in the pew. I recall doodling in my second grade Sunday school class with regularity. I had an absolute blast singing in the children's choir and performing cantatas on a yearly basis. I remember my kind, loving Sunday school teachers and our "old fashion days," where everyone would dress up in vintage clothing, and we would churn apple butter in a giant kettle. I recall our church talent shows fondly and vacation Bible school, church camp, and memorable youth group trips in the summertime.

But as I aged, my participation in my local church waned. At thirteen, I launched into a full-on rebellion and walked out of the church for the next four years. Sure, I'd "go" when Mom required it of me, which was most Sundays, Christmas, and Easter, and I'd hang out with our social youth group in the back pews, but I wasn't spiritually engaged in any form or fashion. I knew most of the Bible's "stories" and did believe in God; at twelve years of age, I even went through "confirmation" but had no relationship with Jesus. To me, in that season of my life, church started at eleven o'clock sharp and ended at twelve o'clock dull.

"Church" just wasn't very interesting or intriguing to me. Aside from the weekly gatherings, I didn't understand what the purpose of going was. Don't get me wrong. The church I grew up in had some of the most amazing people, many of whom I still consider dear friends and some of whom I would say were/are great role models, and a few eventually even became mentors in the faith. But nothing about going to the church nor the services drew me in and made me want to be there on a Sunday or any other day during that rebellious season of my life.

Now, looking back, much of that obviously may have to do with the fact that I did not have a relationship with Jesus, as I mentioned. Some of it may have to do with the fact that there were some stylistic issues with the liturgical services I had trouble engaging with.

I viewed the church as that place you passed on your way to something else, or the place you went to on Sundays and/or special occasions, or that group that people I knew belonged to. In other words, I equated church with *the building, the weekly service/event, or a religious organization.* Even as a young Christian for a while, this is how I viewed church.

Sadly, that is what "church" has devolved into for most Christians: *a building, a service/event or an organization,* or a combination of the three. We "go to church," or we "have church," or people "belong to a church." But is that how the Bible defines "church?"

God's church is not a building (Acts 7:48) or a service. God's church is not an organization, it is a *living organism.*

Sadly, that is what "church" has devolved into for most Christians: a building, a service/event or an organization, or a combination of the three.

The rest of this book is going to challenge your notion of "church." The goal of this book is to present to you the five major foundational identities of the church according to the Bible, and out of those identities, understand and empower the church's purpose.

It is not meant as a *specific* critique or rebuke of any one church, or denomination, or size, or type of church...it is simply looking at the Bible to see how the Scriptures define "church" and then comparing that to what "many churches" are doing in this day and age. If the shoe fits, we must wear it. Or at least own it. But maybe it's time to get a new pair of shoes!

The Old Is Good Enough

Let me illustrate the above point with a teaching from Jesus:

> And He was also telling them a parable: "No one tears a piece of cloth from a new garment and puts it on an old garment; otherwise, he will both tear the new, and the piece from the new will not match the old. And no one puts

new wine into old wineskins; otherwise, the new wine will burst the skins and it will be spilled out, and the skins will be ruined. But new wine must be put into fresh wineskins. And no one, after drinking old wine wishes for new; for he says, 'The old is good enough.'"

Luke 5:37-39

"The old is good enough." Sadly, that is the problem with many churches today. The old wine is good, and the old wineskin still holds the old wine. It's *good enough*. Many times, when we settle for "the good," we miss the "God."

In John 5:19, Jesus said that He only did what He saw His Father doing. We can be doing good things that seemingly are helpful to us and even to those around us and not necessarily be in the center of God's will. We are not just called to be "good Christians" and do "good things," neither as individuals nor as the church.

We are called to partner with God (be "yoked" with Him; Matthew 11:29) and join Him in furthering His kingdom and His will upon the earth (Matthew 6:10). This involves seasons where God wants to bring "new wine," which also will require "new wineskins."

When we get stuck in and even put our confidence in our traditions, patterns, programs, and structures (old wine and old wineskins), we can become rigid and resistant to change. The "old is good enough." Jesus even told the Pharisees that many of their man-made traditions "nullified the word of God" in Mark 7:13.

King Hezekiah had to address similar issues with the Israelites during his reign:

> He removed the high places and broke down the sacred pillars and cut down the Asherah. He also broke in pieces the bronze serpent that Moses had made, for until those days the sons of Israel burned incense to it; and it was called Nehushtan.
>
> 2 Kings 18:4

The "bronze serpent," which was created at God's command to bring healing to the Israelites in the wilderness (Numbers 21), had now become an idol to God's people. King Hezekiah saw the things that were holding Israel back from becoming all that God had purposed it to be, so he was proactive in removing those hindrances.

Sometimes, things that God uses in our past, even things that originated from Him, can become an idol to us in our present. We look to the *thing* that God used instead of looking to God Himself.

Sometimes, things that God uses in our past, even things that originated from Him, can become an idol to us in our present. We look to the *thing* that God used instead of looking to God Himself.

The reality is that God often uses change to change us. He knows that we are creatures of habit, so, often, He allows us to encounter change out of necessity. Since He has predestined us to be conformed to the image of His Son (Romans 8:29), He will use all the circumstances in our lives for our and His good (Romans 8:28). This includes times and seasons where He leads us and moves us to places outside our comfort zones.

> You shall remember all the way which the LORD your God has led you in the wilderness these forty years, that He might humble you, testing you, to know what was in your heart, whether you would keep His commandments or not.
>
> Deuteronomy 8:2

God's plan was to get Israel out of Egypt and into the promised land, but He used the time in the wilderness to get "Egypt" out of them and change them from slaves into an army. He also used that time to reveal their hearts. Even then, a whole generation perished because they refused to change. The Bible even says that the Spirit "led" Jesus into the wilderness. If you look at it in the original Greek text in the Book of Mark, it can be translated as "the Spirit *cast* Jesus into the wilderness" (Mark 1:12; emphasis mine). Sometimes, the Holy Spirit leads us into uncomfortable places and seasons.

As an individual and as a church, are you open to change? Are you willing to get outside your comfort zones? Are you willing to address any ministry idols, and are you open to honestly assessing your traditions? Are you ready for "new wine" and "new wineskins?"

Violation of Divine Design

I'd say it's a pretty general consensus that most Christians have a negative image of the Pharisees, and for a good reason. However, even though they did have a host of issues that prevented them from recognizing Jesus as their Messiah, God still reached out to them with opportunities for repentance, even right as Jesus appeared on the scene.

God sent a strange man named John the Baptist to call the nation of Israel to repentance, including the Pharisees. But John was bringing "new wine" (his message), and he himself was definitely a "new wineskin."

Now in those days John the Baptist came, preaching in the wilderness of Judea, saying, "Repent, for the kingdom of heaven is at hand." For this is the one referred to by Isaiah the prophet when he said, "THE VOICE OF

ON CRYING IN THE WILDERNESS, 'MAKE READY THE WAY OF THE LORD, MAKE HIS PATHS STRAIGHT!'"

Now John himself had a garment of camel's hair and a leather belt around his waist; and his food was locusts and wild honey. Then Jerusalem was going out to him, and all Judea and all the district around the Jordan; and they were being baptized by him in the Jordan River, as they confessed their sins.

But when he saw many of the Pharisees and Sadducees coming for baptism, he said to them, "You brood of vipers, who warned you to flee from the wrath to come? *Therefore, bear fruit in keeping with repentance;* and do not suppose that you can say to yourselves, 'We have Abraham for our father'; for I say to you that from these stones God is able to raise up children to Abraham. The axe is already laid at the root of the trees; therefore, every tree that does not bear good fruit is cut down and thrown into the fire.

"As for me, I baptize you with water for repentance, but He who is coming after me is mightier than I, and I am not fit to remove His sandals; He will baptize you with the Holy Spirit and fire. His winnowing fork is in His hand, and

He will thoroughly clear His threshing floor;
and He will gather His wheat into the barn,
but He will burn up the chaff with unquench-
able fire."

Matthew 3:1-12 (emphasis mine)

Now, John came preaching repentance because of
the next Messenger who was soon to be on the scene,
his cousin Jesus; he was "preparing the way of the Lord"
(Isaiah 40:3, 4).

Most Christians probably believe that God had already made up His mind about the Pharisees and had
washed His hands of them, but actually, God sent John
for the Pharisees too: "But the Pharisees and the law-
yers *rejected God's purpose for themselves*, not having been
baptized by John" (Luke 7:30; emphasis mine).

Let this sink in: God gave the Pharisees an opportunity to join with Him in what He was about to do,
and it was His purpose for them, but they rejected the
opportunity, in large part, because they had a misunderstanding about their own identity (Luke 3:8), but
mainly because they were unwilling to change. They
were satisfied with the status quo.

What happens when we refuse to change when God
is asking us to change so that we can partner with His
purpose is that He often allows the change to come to
us.

"Moab has been at ease since his youth; He has also been undisturbed, like wine on its dregs, And he has not been emptied from vessel to vessel, Nor has he gone into exile. Therefore he retains his flavor, And his aroma has not changed. Therefore behold, the days are coming," declares the LORD, "when I will send to him those who tip vessels, and they will tip him over, and they will empty his vessels and shatter his jars."

Jeremiah 48:10-12

As I read this teaching and description from Rick Joyner many years ago, it had a profound impact on my life in understanding how important change is:

What God is describing in these verses is the process of wine purification in those days. Wine would be poured from "vessel to vessel," allowing for the sediments which had come to rest on the bottom to remain in the first vessel as it was poured into the second one. Then the same process would be followed until there was almost no sediment (impurifications) left.

If we don't allow ourselves to be poured from vessel to vessel, then we are in danger of having our vessels tipped over and our jars shattered. This is both true of us individually, as well as corporately. (See "Preparation for Ministry" by Rick Joyner, *The MorningStar Journal*, Volumes 1.1 and 1.2.)

As I said earlier, God uses change to change us.

The Scriptures tell us that God is coming back for a bride (the church; see chapters *"The* Foundational Identity: Family" & "The Family's Purpose: Love") without a spot or wrinkle (Ephesians 5:27), and so He must help the *bride* to make herself ready (Revelation 19:7).

God uses change to change us.

We often look at the truth of what is spoken in the Scriptures as something God wants to convey to us as individuals, but the reality is there is much in the Bible that speaks specifically to "the church." All of Paul's letters were written to a corporate body ("To the Saints [plural] at Ephesus," to the Saints at Philippi, etc.), and the letters in the Book of Revelation were addressing the corporate body as well.

God has purposes (Isaiah 46:10; Acts 13:36) and plans for us (Jeremiah 29:11-14; Ephesians 2:10; Psalm 33:11), and they are intricately tied to our identity, both individually and corporately.

When we allow the church to become or operate as anything other than what God created it to be, it is a *violation of divine design*. There are things we do when we gather corporately that are not necessarily "biblical" in the truest sense of the word, and yet, it may indeed still produce spiritual fruit; *but...*are we on a path or course that will allow the church to be and fulfill *all* that God has desired, planned, and purposed for it to be and fulfill?

When we allow the church to become or operate as anything other than what God created it to be, it is a violation of divine design.

As you will read in the chapter "Identity Empowers Purpose," we must first understand and begin to operate in our true identities before we can be empowered to *fully* walk in our God-given purpose.

I describe the church in America's current state as "modern Americanized Christianity." Not only have we arrived at a place and time where most Christians (and most non-believers) in this country equate church with *a building, a service/event, or an organization,* we've exported this concept to a great portion of the world through missions. Why are pastors in Africa wearing three-piece suits to preach in on Sunday mornings at 11 a.m.?

Some segments of our modern church culture have turned church into a social club, while some see it primarily as a social justice organization. Some have turned church into a means of accumulating wealth, and others have turned church into a venue of entertainment. Some churches are still walking in manmade traditions of past generations and are speaking a language that is foreign to those in our current culture.

There are *many* issues that we could debate endlessly about, as to the nuances of what kind of service to have, and we could also talk about the latest, greatest program, paradigms, focus, or fads.

But instead of doing that, in this book, I want to focus mainly on who God has said the church is. God is the Creator and Designer of all we see. He made all of creation with plans and a purpose. After all, He designed it. He created it. He decided on its identity, and He laid out the plans and purpose that He has for it. It's all right there in the Bible if we'll only look.

When you think of "the church," what do you equate it with? Do you think of the church as *a building, a service/event, or an organization?* Maybe even in your head, you have a definition that lines up more with what the Bible says, but does it translate to how your church *actually* functions? Or how you function in relation to your church?

Let me clarify by stating that when I refer to the church, I am referring to the true church (*ecclesia* in the original Greek text) spoken of in Scripture that is made up of born-again believers that encompasses the whole earth. I am not talking about random groups of people who have memberships in religious institutions or people who claim to be believers simply because their parents went to church or they "believe in God."

Not one church or a specific local church (although that would still be generally true), but *the* church, meaning the universal church made up of the members of the *body* of Christ worldwide.

In this book, I will lay out the five major foundational identities of the church found in the Scriptures and show you how they work within God's design to bring about God's fullness and His purpose for the church so that it can fulfill its destiny.

I invite you to look up the Scriptures for yourself (Acts 17:11) and ask the Holy Spirit to lead you into all truth and teach you all things (John 14:26, 16:13; 1 John 2:27), and let God's truth be established (Romans 3:4).

But as I said, be ready to be challenged!

"If the Foundations are Destroyed, What Can the Righteous Do?" (Psalm 11:3)

Foundations are extremely important in the economy of God. Probably one of the most well-known parables Jesus ever taught illustrates this importance:

> Therefore, everyone who hears these words of Mine and acts on them, may be compared to a wise man who built his house on the rock. And the rain fell, and the floods came, and the winds blew and slammed against that house; and yet it did not fall, for it had been founded on the rock. Everyone who hears these words of Mine and does not act on them, will be

like a foolish man who built his house on the sand. The rain fell, and the floods came, and the winds blew and slammed against that house; and it fell—and great was its fall.

Matthew 7:24-27

Are our foundations of how we see and operate as the church built upon the rock (of Jesus and His Word), or are they built upon shifting sands of modern church culture and/or religious tradition?

Are our foundations of how we see and operate as the church built upon the rock (of Jesus and His Word), or are they built upon shifting sands of modern church culture and/or religious tradition?

The apostle Paul also realized the importance of a good foundation:

According to the grace of God which was given to me, *like a wise master builder I laid a foundation, and another is building on it. But each man must be careful how he builds on it. For no man can lay a foundation other than the one which is laid, which is Jesus Christ.* Now if any

28

man builds on the foundation with gold, silver, precious stones, wood, hay, straw, each man's work will become evident; for the day will show it because it is to be revealed with fire, and the fire itself will test the quality of each man's work. If any man's work which he has built on it remains, he will receive a reward. If any man's work is burned up, he will suffer loss; but he himself will be saved, yet so as through fire.

1 Corinthians 3:10-15 (emphasis mine)

God wants us to build on solid foundations, His foundations. What we build on those foundations may vary, but it is important that we lay proper foundations if what we build should last and produce the lasting fruit that God desires (John 15:16).

The Temple (2 Chronicles 6) and the Tabernacle (Exodus 26) before it were designed by God with specific, detailed instructions that were not to be deviated from. Exact measurements, precise details were given to Moses for the Tabernacle and to David for what was to become Solomon's Temple.

In the same way, God has specific designs for His church (as one of the five major foundational identities of the church is *the temple*), how it is to be built, and the foundation that it is to be built upon. So, in light of that, let's look at the five major foundational identities of the church:

1. The *family*
2. The *bride*
3. The *body*
4. The *temple*
5. The *army*

The apostle Paul mentions two of these major identities in Ephesians 2:19-21 (emphasis mine):

> So then, you are no longer strangers and aliens, but you are fellow citizens with the saints, and are *of God's household*, having been built on the foundation of the apostles and prophets, Christ Jesus Himself being the corner stone, in whom the whole building, being fitted together, is growing into a *holy temple* in the Lord...

We'll discuss the *family* (household of God) in chapters "The Foundational Identity: Family" & "The Family's Purpose: Love" and the *temple* as an identity more in chapters "The Fourth Identity: Temple" & "The Temple's Purpose: Glory," but I wanted you to see the correlation between how God builds and grows His church and the foundation that it is being built upon.

Jesus is the Cornerstone and the Capstone. He is the beginning and the end, the Alpha and Omega. He is also our Firstborn Brother in *the family* (Romans 8:29b; Hebrews 2:11). He is the Groom to *the bride* (Matthew 9:15). He is the *head of the body* (Ephesians 4:15). He is the Great High Priest in *the temple* (Hebrews 4:14-16). He is the King of Kings and Captain of the Host who leads *the army* (Revelation 19:11-16).

Jesus is the center, the focus, the foundation of everything we do as the church. He desires to have first place.

"He is also *head of the body, the church*; and He is the beginning, the firstborn from the dead, *so that He Himself will come to have first place in everything*" (Colossians 1:18; emphasis mine).

Christianity is not a religion. It is not a belief system. It is, at its core, a relationship with God the Father, through Jesus His Son, made possible and empowered by the Holy Spirit living within us. We have this relationship as individuals *and* as His church.

As we are connected to (John 15:5) and focused on Jesus, both individually and corporately as the church *and* we walk in His designed identities, we will experience the life He promised (1 John 5:12; John 10:10b) and fulfill His purposes.

Identity Empowers Purpose

As Christians, we do not "do to become," we do because of "who we already are."

Let me explain what I mean when I say that.

We don't do to become (work or perform to establish our identity), we do *out of* who we already are (our already given, established biblical identity), who God says we are.

Performing or striving to obtain an identity is what I refer to as "performance-based acceptance" or PBA for short. Those with this mindset often are trying to work to gain a more spiritual identity or working to gain acceptance from God.

It's not unlike the Catholic view that says you have to have accomplished three miracles to be considered a "saint." Well, God already considers you a saint, according to the Bible. Paul addressed most of his letters (epistles) to the saints at the specific city-churches he was addressing: "To the saints at Philippi," "To the saints at Colossae," etc.

The word "saint" simply means "holy one." Jesus did all the work on the cross that was necessary for God to consider you "holy." Do we still have a sinful nature? Yes. Do we still sin? Yes. Does that change how God sees us? No. Because He sees us through the filter of the blood and finished work of His Son.

Proverbs 23:7a says, "As he thinks within himself, so he is" (cf. Proverbs 27:19).

If you see yourself as and take on the identity of a sinner in your life, what will you continue to do with regularity? Sin. There is a difference between seeing yourself as a sinner who struggles with holiness versus a saint who occasionally sins. It is a big difference, and it is an *important* difference.

God accepts you because of the finished work of the cross, and there is nothing you can do to make Him accept you more, and there is nothing you can do to make Him accept you less.

The same is true of your God-given identity. You are a new creation (2 Corinthians 5:17) with a new identity. The old has passed away.

In Judges, chapter six, we see the well-known story of Gideon: "Israel was brought very low because of Midian, and the sons of Israel cried to the LORD" (v. 6).

We find the soon-to-be hero of this story, Gideon, hiding in a winepress beating out wheat because he was afraid of the Midianites. When the angel of the Lord shows up to greet him, he greets Gideon by saying, "The Lord is with you, O valiant warrior!"

But wait just a second...Gideon was cowering in a winepress because of fear. He wasn't a skilled and seasoned warrior like King David. He hadn't proven himself in battle, yet the identity he had been given by the messenger of heaven was that he was a *valiant warrior.*

His revealed identity as a valiant warrior was meant to empower his purpose that was to deliver Israel from the oppression of Midian, which he did.

For another example, let's look at Jesus in Matthew, chapters three and four. In Matthew 3:16, 17, immediately after Jesus was baptized by John the Baptist, He received this declaration over Himself from God His Father: "This is My beloved Son, with whom I am well pleased."

Jesus is affirmed in His identity as the Son. And even though Jesus had yet to do one single miracle or healing, His Father says to Him that He is well pleased! The Father's pleasure in His Son had nothing to do with Jesus's performance; it had to do with Who He was!

He then heads into the wilderness, where He is tempted by the devil. What are the points of attack on

Jesus? His identity: "If you are the Son...[do this]" (Matthew 4:3; 4:6).

Of course, we know that Jesus answered each temptation with the truth of the Word of God ("It is written..."), standing in agreement with what His Father had declared over Him. He didn't have to perform or prove or obtain His identity by doing something. He simply needed to believe what His Father said (John 13:3).

Let's look at two individual biblical identities and how we can operate out of them in a healthy way and a less healthy way:

The Bible refers to us as sons/daughters of God (His children) and also as servants (bond servants: Acts 4:29; 2 Corinthians 4:5; Galatians 1:10). Both of these are biblical identities and good for us to operate in, *but how* we operate in them (progression) is important!

If we take on and operate out of the identity as a servant first, then we may have a tendency to try and please God through performance (or works, PBA). However, as we mentioned above, we do not do to become; we do out of who we already are (identity) and Who we are in relation with Him (John 5:19).

"The slave [servant] does not remain in the house forever; the son does remain forever" (John 8:35).

"No longer do I call you slaves [servants], for the slave does not know what his Master is doing" (John 15:15).

As sons and daughters, we have an inheritance that is not earned but freely given. We don't have to perform because Jesus already did the work on the cross necessary for us to be accepted and to receive an inheritance. We come to God boldly and with confidence because Jesus made the way for us, and the character of our Father is such that He accepts us, even with our flaws and failures.

The prodigal son was still a son when he returned and had the full measure of his sonship restored, even though in his own mind he was only worthy of being a hired servant. A son or daughter knows that their relationship is secure because of their identity as a child of the Father.

I remember two times in my life that I went through my personal identity crises. During the time when Blockbuster (the video store chain) ruled the world, I worked at a local video store in my small hometown. I had worked my way all the way up to manager. Many people knew me by name, but some folks just knew me as the "video guy."

I didn't realize how much of my identity was wrapped up in that title until I left that job. All of a sudden, I was thinking, *Who am I, now that I'm no longer an important person at the video store?* I've seen many people take on the identity of their work or career.

A few years later, I was the lead singer of a Christian band that had gained a small amount of attention around the globe. I can honestly tell you: I thought that was what I would do for the rest of my life. I had put so much of my identity in that role that when the band broke up, I again was in another identity crisis.

God wants us to have our identities established in Him because His identities are eternal. They never change. I'm a son now, and I'll be a son when I get to heaven.

The devil attacks our identity because he does not want us to be empowered to live out of these declared identities and truths over our lives, nor walk in the promises and purposes God has for us. As individuals, we are more than conquerors, overcomers, and so much more according to the Word of God. Knowing *who* we are *empowers* what we are called to *do* (purpose). The same is true of our identity as the church.

God wants us to have our identities established in Him because His identities are eternal. They never change.

The five major foundational identities of the church are the corporate versions of the major individual identities we share as individual believers:

1. sons/daughters (children),
2. saints (betrothed "holy ones" in covenant relationship),
3. members of His *body*,
4. temples of the Holy Spirit/living stones,
5. soldiers.

Since we are all sons and daughters (2 Corinthians 6:18), that means we all have the same Father and are a part of the same *family*. Since we are all enlisted soldiers (2 Timothy 2:3, 4), then we are a part of the same *army*, etc.

The personal identities that God gives us are important for us to be able to walk in victory and fulfill the purpose and plans that God has for each one of us as individuals. And likewise, the identities He has given the church are important for us to understand and walk in to be spiritually victorious and fulfill the purpose and plans that God has for us together, corporately, as His church.

Currently, some in our modern Americanized Christian culture view church as optional. Some think church is there to meet our needs, and if they don't like how it is done, they stop giving or stop serving, or go somewhere else or don't go at all. Sure, there have been scandals, poor models, bad examples, even abuse. But those things do not invalidate God's identities and design. As they say, "Don't throw the baby out with the bath water."

God did not design church to be optional, but rather He designed the church in such a way that we could not function effectively or mature fully apart from it! The old adage is true: there are no lone rangers in the kingdom of God.

> **God did not design church to be optional, but rather He designed the church in such a way that we could not function effectively or mature fully apart from it!**

But speaking the truth in love, we are to grow up in all aspects into Him who is the head, even Christ, from whom *the whole body, being fitted and held together by what every joint supplies, according to the proper working of each individual part, causes the growth of the body for the building up of itself in love.*

Ephesians 4:15-17 (emphasis mine)

"One who separates himself seeks his own desire; He quarrels against all sound wisdom" (Proverbs 18:1).

Our lack of commitment to the church only reveals our lack of understanding of the church as God has designed it. And again, the leadership of modern Americanized Christianity shares some responsibility for this mess because we have not presented a biblical understanding of the identity and purpose of the church as it is laid out in the Scriptures, nor modeled our churches to function in them.

Just as God wants us to walk in our individual identities, which will empower the purposes of God in our individual lives, He desires that the church would walk in its foundational identities so that it may be empowered to walk out the purposes that God has destined for it.

Ezra, Nehemiah, and the Five Major Foundational Identities of the Church

In the book of Ezra, we see the return of the Jewish remnant, led by Ezra, the priest, from the seventy-year Babylonian captivity to rebuild the Temple in Jerusalem. He also led the remnant in renewing their covenant with God.

In the book of Nehemiah, we see a story of God's people rebuilding the city of Jerusalem that lay in ruins. Nehemiah has the vision for the completed work, but it takes God's people, in the face of opposition, working together to rebuild the city.

To me, in these two books, there is the closest picture of how the New Testament church is supposed to operate that we find in the Old Testament. I believe as we look closely at how this story plays out, we can see facets of all five of the major foundational identities of the church.

In Nehemiah, we see glimpses of the *family*, the *body*, and the *army*. In Ezra, we see the *bride* and the *temple*. It is important to remember that the Old Testament is the New concealed and the New Testament is the Old revealed.

The Bible is not two separate archives of history: one Jewish, the other Christian. It is one continuous story of God's redemptive purposes in the earth and His desire to have an eternal family and to have a relationship with them. Contrary to what some are teaching in the *body* of Christ, the Old Testament does not take a backseat to the New.

There are certain types, foreshadows, and pictures of things to come throughout the Old Testament. There are Messianic figures (Moses, David), there is a Pentecost-like outpouring (Numbers 11:24-29), and a slew of other things that give us a glimpse into what we see come in *fullness* in the New Testament (Colossians 2:17).

But just as faith (the word translated as "trust" from Hebrew) has always been the currency in God's economy (see Hebrews 11) in both the Old and New Testaments, we can also see God's heart for His people and how He desired they relate to Himself and to each other, in both Testaments.

The nation of Israel was made up of tribes. Each tribe had different abilities and skills. Each tribe was comprised of families, and each family was comprised of individuals.

We see God's design and His desire play out in the story of Ezra and Nehemiah and the rebuilding of the Temple and the walls around the city of Jerusalem. If you need to acquaint or reacquaint yourself with these two books, by all means, set this book down and grab your Bible.

We'll take a brief look at the five major foundational identities of the church in relation to the biblical narrative in these two books.

The Family/Household of God

Nehemiah recognized the importance of family. The Jewish people, even in the modern day, in general, have placed an incredibly high value on this God-ordained institution. When Nehemiah set off to Jerusalem to "rebuild the walls," he understood this was not his only task; he was also rebuilding a people.

Most of the Jewish people had been in captivity, and everything they knew was then in ruins. Nehemiah could have asked the King for builders, but he knew the work needed to be done by the people who had a vested interest in it.

To overcome all the difficulties they faced, Nehemiah had them work as families (Nehemiah 4). He helped them see that they were all brothers and sisters (Nehemiah 5) and they needed to treat each other as family. They had to come together and work through stressful, difficult, and, yes, even dangerous circumstances.

Let's say someone you know who is a believer goes to a different church. How do you see them? Do you see them as a person who believes a different doctrine? Do you see them as a member of an incompatible congregation? Or do you view them as a brother or sister in the Lord? We are all family.

The Bride

During this process of rebuilding, Ezra rediscovers "the Law," and the people renew their covenant relationship by agreeing to live in accordance with the Scriptures.

The people of Ezra's and Nehemiah's time had intermarried with foreign wives, made political alliances with the enemies of Israel and had strayed from, and even forgotten the commands of Scripture. They were called to repent of these sins and get back to God's design for living in accordance with His Word.

We, as the people of God, are going to need to get back to the Word of God as it relates to and defines the church. Remember, as previously mentioned: *the church is not a building, an event/service, or an organization.* We may have some things to repent of as well.

Where have outside influences affected how we conduct our affairs? Where have we made unrighteous alliances? How have we strayed from the Word? Just like those in the days of Ezra and Nehemiah, we may need consecration.

The Body

To rebuild both the Temple and the walls surrounding Jerusalem, everybody had to participate. Everybody had to do their part. *Entire families* took part in the building process. No one was a spectator in these projects.

Just like in Nehemiah, we all have to do our part in what God has designed. We are not called to sit on the sideline (or in the pew), spectate, and just receive. We co-labor with God in the growing, maturing, and building of His church. We have to take our place "at the wall."

The people of God were committed to not only the task but to each other. They were living out this prophecy from the Book of Isaiah: "Those from among you will rebuild the ancient ruins; You will raise up the age-old foundations; And you will be called the repairer of the breach, the restorer of the streets in which to dwell" (Isaiah 58:12).

Are we committed to what God wants to build within His church? It will take all of us doing our part, not just being "members of an organization," but being functioning members of a living organism.

The church grows as we as individuals do our part (Ephesians 4:15, 16). We supply our time. We supply our treasures. We supply our talents. We are there to give, not just get. But this is so much more than volunteering in our faith communities or at our houses of worship.

In our assemblies, one person, one pastor, or one leader was never meant to do it all. They can't do it all. The church was designed to be a *body ministry*. It even goes way beyond paid staff and monthly volunteers.

Nehemiah couldn't do all the work himself. He and his servants couldn't do it. It took everyone to rebuild the Temple, to rebuild the walls. And when it was done, it wasn't just the structures that were rebuilt, nor a city, but a people.

The Temple

The Temple was the center point of the worship of the Jewish people in those days. If they did not live close enough to the Temple to go there, they would pray towards Jerusalem because that's where the Temple was.

And in the Temple, in the Holy of Holies, were the Ark of the Covenant and the presence of God.

After being in exile, the people of God needed to be re-established in their promised land, complete with their prescribed spiritual practices.

Ezra not only led the effort of reacquainting the people with the Book of the Law (the Word of God), but He also led the effort in rebuilding the Temple and re-establishing the priesthood and their ceremonial practices (Ezra 3; Nehemiah 8).

We, as the modern church, have been in "exile" and haven't even realized it. We, in a lot of respects, have been taken captive by our culture. We need to be reacquainted with God's Word as it relates to His church and His prescribed design of it and the practices He has commanded us to walk in.

The Army

When Nehemiah, in chapter four of the book of the same name, was overseeing the repairs of the burnt gates and broken-down walls, he was aware that these places were weak spots where the enemies of God's people could get in and cause harm. He stationed families there, with a tool in one hand and a weapon in the other.

Not all, probably not many, who helped rebuild the gates and the wall were actual craftsmen, artisans, or builders. But they all helped build. Even fewer were trained warriors and fighters, but they were willing to fight.

Did you know there was actually a tribe in Israel that was ambidextrous?

"They were equipped with bows, using both the right hand and the left to sling stones and to shoot arrows from the bow; they were Saul's kinsmen from Benjamin" (1 Chronicles 12:2).

This should bring to mind this related scripture: "... commending ourselves as Servants of God [...] in the word of truth, in the power of God; by the weapons of righteousness for the right hand and the left" (2 Corinthians 6:4a, 7).

Those from the tribe of Benjamin weren't just able to use both hands to fight; they were experts who were trained to do so! God wants to train us in the same way for us to fight in the spiritual realm.

"He trains my hands for battle, so that my arms can bend a bow of bronze" (2 Samuel 22:35; Psalm 18:34).

"Blessed be the Lord, my rock, who trains my hands for war, And my fingers for battle" (Psalm 144:1).

He trains us as individual soldiers so that we can fight in and as an army.

Are you willing to see your fellow saints as brothers and sisters? Are you willing to reconsecrate yourselves? Are you willing to work alongside others to accomplish

God's work? Are you willing to return to God's design for worship? Are you willing to fight for your brothers and sisters?

There is much to take away from these two Old Testament books. My prayer is that the universal church will relearn, return and rebuild its age-old foundations.

The Purposes and Corresponding Traits

As we've learned previously, identity empowers purpose. Walking in who we are helps us to walk out what we are called to do. These five identities of the church are given to us to help us walk out what we are called to do as the church.

The five major identities of the church are foundational and progressive:

1. The *family/household* of God
2. The *bride* of Christ
3. The *body* of Christ
4. The *temple* of God
5. The *army* of God

Every identity of the church runs parallel to an individual identity that we already walk in:

1. Family: we are individually sons & daughters of God (His children).
2. The bride of Christ: we are individually already in covenant relationship as "saints" (holy ones).
3. The body of Christ: we are individually "members of His body."
4. The temple of God: we are individually "living stones" and temples of the Holy Spirit.
5. The army of God: we are individually "soldiers."

Also, each identity of the church has a trait and/or emphasis that corresponds to it. These are the "purpose" of each of these major identities:

1. Family = love
2. The bride of Christ = purity
3. The body of Christ = unity
4. The temple of God = glory
5. The army of God = power

The *progression* of these five major foundational identities of the church is very important as well. Each identity builds on the prior one. When we learn how to operate in each prior identity, it molds us, prepares us, and empowers us to be successful in the next identity.

Many in the modern church want to shoot right for the top and be a "victorious *army*," and they want to go to war with the enemy on any and all battlegrounds. And we should want to walk in the power of God and to see victories in our churches, in our workplaces, in our neighborhoods, and in our cities and regions!

God wants us to be victorious too, but He has designed it in such a way that major victories in the spirit realm come through the church, not individuals; and when we skip the vital and foundational identities of the church that come before being an army, we miss the key ingredients, if you will, that make the recipe work for the church *becoming* and *walking* as a victorious army.

There is a *big* difference between being an individual soldier in God's army and walking, working together, and winning as the army. Soldiers don't win major battles or wars by themselves; armies do.

But armies go through a *lot of training together* to be combat-ready.

Most churches are also very comfortable operating in the middle identity, *the body*. It is a very "functional" identity. But then again, it can become very dysfunctional if we skip the first two foundational identities that are building blocks to this third identity, as we will see when we discuss them all in detail in the coming chapters.

As the church, we cannot "cherry-pick" the identities we want to be and operate in, just as you cannot put a second floor on a building that has no solid foundation and first-story walls to support it.

We are going to look at each of these individually in greater detail in the coming chapters, but I wanted to give a brief overview of each purpose in relation to its corresponding identity.

The *family* identity is where we learn to love. Loving the way God has commanded, not the way we think we ought, whoever we think deserves it or has earned it.

"A new command I give you: Love one another. As I have loved you, so you must love one another" (John 13:34).

The *bride* is where we learn purity. Jesus is coming back for a bride without a spot or wrinkle. We can't make ourselves holy and pure, but we can yield to the Spirit's work in us to purify us.

"...and to present her to himself as a radiant church, without stain or wrinkle or any other blemish, but holy and blameless" (Ephesians 5:27).

The *body* is where we learn unity. Unity is a powerful force in the spiritual realm. When we come together in agreement, despite our differences, God can do amazing things in us and through us.

I appeal to you, brothers and sisters, in the name of our Lord Jesus Christ, that all of you agree with one another in what you say and

> that there be no divisions among you, but that
> you be perfectly united in mind and thought.
>
> 1 Corinthians 1:10 (NIV)

The *temple* is where we can both see and receive God's glory. There are two types of God's glory: His manifest presence and His thoughts, opinions, and recognition of who we are. The manifest presence of God changes us as individuals, and it also changes us as a corporate body. Understanding God's thoughts, opinions, and recognition of who He created us to be are paramount to our walking in His declared identities of us, both individually and corporately.

"But we all, with unveiled face, beholding as in a mirror the glory of the Lord, are being transformed into the same image from glory to glory, just as from the Lord, the Spirit" (2 Corinthians 3:18).

The *army* is where we walk in God's power. Just as we read about in Ezra and Nehemiah, as an army, we want to fight for each other and fight alongside each other. We want to see the kingdom of God advanced and established and see the enemy displaced and vanquished. Our battles are in the spiritual realm, and to win them fully, we must fight as His church.

"...so that the manifold wisdom of God might now be made known *through the church* to the rulers and the authorities in the heavenly places" (Ephesians 3:10; emphasis mine).

As we walk in all of the identities and walk out all of their purposes, we will allow God to position us to be His victorious end-times *army*!

The Foundational Identity: Family

We already know that this is *the* foundational identity of the church. God created us to be in a relationship with Him, not in a religion. God has chosen *family* as the primary structure for the relationship. We are His children (sons & daughters), and He has recreated this structure in the earthly realm, both in the natural and in the Spirit.

You may have heard the phrase, "Blood is thicker than water," describing the idea that family comes before any other relationship. This is true in the kingdom as well. God has an "order." Inside of the natural family, there is an order: spousal relationship comes before the relationship with children. It is similar in our kingdom family:

"So then, while we have opportunity, let us do good to all people, and *especially to those who are of the household of the faith*" (Galatians 6:10; emphasis mine).

But we are painfully divided into camps, competing organizations, and denominations in the worldwide church. We are much more factions than family.

Instead of loving, serving, encouraging, and helping each other, we fight, argue, publicly denounce and malign one another in the name of the Lord. These things ought not to be! (See James 3:9-12.)

But we are painfully divided into camps, competing organizations, and denominations in the worldwide church. We are much more factions than family.

The problem that many of us have is that our family situations are or have not been an ideal example of what a healthy family dynamic looks like. It could be dysfunction in the household we grew up in; it could be an incomplete family structure that keeps us from experiencing some family relationships and dynamics that we need in order to know how to interact with family members in a positive way. Divorce, estranged relationships, abuse, abandonment...these things keep us from experiencing healthy family dynamics and relationships. This high rate of dysfunctionality in our natural families has been brought into our spiritual family.

This sets us up to struggle with relationships within our new spiritual family. *Hurting people hurt people.* This is why it's important for us to deal with our family history and current family relationships (even past spiritual family relationships) in a biblical manner so that we can begin to walk in healthy family dynamics and relationships.

The devil will make sure that you are hurt in relationships: whether it is someone in authority (parents or pastors) or a close relationship where you allowed yourself to be vulnerable and experienced betrayal or something very painful in the context of a relationship.

The devil does this on purpose because he wants you to live in distrust of people, especially those within your natural and spiritual families. He wants you to have walls up, to be suspicious of people's motives and intentions, to be quick to anger and slow to forgive.

Unforgiveness is one of the devil's biggest traps, and it has ensnared many. Have you ever noticed that the Lord's Prayer is in the context of dealing with forgiveness?

> Pray, then, in this way: "Our Father who is in heaven, hallowed be Your name. Your kingdom come. Your will be done, On earth as it is in heaven. Give us this day our daily bread. And forgive us our debts, as we also have for-

given our debtors. And do not lead us into temptation, but deliver us from evil. [For Yours is the kingdom and the power and the glory forever. Amen.]"
For if you forgive others for their transgressions, your heavenly Father will also forgive you. But if you do not forgive others, then your Father will not forgive your transgressions.
Matthew 6:9-15 (brackets added from NKJV)

So, when Jesus modeled this prayer, He told us to forgive those who sinned against us, and then afterward, He spoke about forgiveness again. Sandwiched right in the middle is "lead us not into temptation, but deliver us from [the evil one]."

Most of us have probably thought this was a general "God, don't let us be tempted" prayer, but it's not. Firstly, because temptation is a given in this world (James 1:13-15); and secondly, because it's in the context of forgiveness.

What Jesus is specifically pointing to here is: "Let us not be tempted to hold unforgiveness and deliver us from the devil's scheme to trap us with unforgiveness."

Many a people is *still* walking with church hurts that they have not released to God in the courtroom of heaven. You may have heard the old adage: holding unforgiveness is like drinking poison and expecting the other person to die. You can choose to be bitter, or you can choose to be better.

We will need to forgive and let God heal our hearts and trust that He will bring about justice if it is needed (Luke 18:7, 8). Otherwise, we will have a closed (hardened) heart, and we won't be able to walk in vulnerability and transparency in our relationships. In some situations, we will need to repent and seek reconciliation.

Jesus modeled this for us in John, chapter thirteen. At the Last Supper (a Passover meal) with His disciples, Jesus washes the feet of those who would betray, deny, and abandon Him, knowing that they would do these things. Would you or I be able to do the same?

We are not just called to be the "us four and no more" family either. Despite our doctrinal differences, our political leanings, and our visions for how to do ministry, we must learn to love one another the way Jesus commanded.

"By this all men will know that you are My disciples, if you have love for one another" (John 13:35).

The Family's Purpose: Love

What does it look like to be a family? We know that we are to be compelled and governed by *love*. We know that it is agape love (unconditional, sacrificial, and selfless) that we are to walk in, demonstrate. God calls us to love each other and to even love our enemies. It's a tall order. We cannot do it in and of ourselves. We obviously must receive this love from God first before we can pass it along to others (1 John 4:19).

In the identity and dynamic of the family, God teaches us, trains us, and helps us learn how to love well. The hard truth is that God has called us to love people who sometimes are hard to love in our own strength.

It's in this foundational identity of the family that God develops His *agape* love: first in us, then through us.

Church should be a safe place to practice, to fail, and even to fall. I know it has not been that for countless people, myself included. As it has been said, the church is the only army that shoots its wounded, and this is a very sad commentary on our modern church culture.

How are we supposed to demonstrate love to a hurting, dying, and broken world when we can't even do it amongst our own "family?"

This is the only starting point of where we are supposed to be living out love. I find it incredibly grievous that the universal church and its members are continually at war with itself and the world is watching. If we can't love well where it should be easy to love, then we will never make it to this place:

> You have heard that it was said, "YOU SHALL LOVE YOUR NEIGHBOR and hate your enemy." But I say to you, *love your enemies and pray for those who persecute you, so that you may prove yourselves to be sons of your Father who is in heaven;* for He causes His sun to rise on the evil and the good, and sends rain on the righteous and the unrighteous. *For if you love those who love you, what reward do you have?* Even the tax collectors, do they not do the same? And if you greet only your brothers and sisters, what more are you doing than others? Even the Gentiles, do they not do the same? Therefore,

you shall be perfect, as your heavenly Father
is perfect.

> Matthew 5:43-48 (emphasis mine)

The entire fifth chapter of Matthew is an indictment
on the universal church. We love to quote it, teach it,
and preach it, but it is very rarely lived out within the
church with regularity. Notice that the context of the
above-quoted passage is *family*.

How are we supposed to demonstrate love to a hurting, dying, and broken world when we can't even do it amongst our own "family?"

This family/love foundation is *the* foundational
identity and trait and helps us to be able to function
effectively and walk in our purposes in the other four
foundations.

"But now faith, hope, and love remain, these three;
but the greatest of these is love" (1 Corinthians 13:13; emphasis mine).

What does love look like pragmatically? Here is love
in action:

> And all those who had believed were together
> and had all things in common; and they be-

gan selling their property and possessions and were sharing them with all, as anyone might have need. Day by day continuing with one mind in the temple, and breaking bread from house to house, they were taking their meals together with gladness and sincerity of heart, praising God and having favor with all the people. And the Lord was adding to their number day by day those who were being saved.

Acts 2:44-47

Jesus demonstrated it this way:

Now before the Feast of the Passover, Jesus knowing that His hour had come that He would depart out of this world to the Father, having loved His own who were in the world, He loved them to the end. During supper, the devil having already put into the heart of Judas Iscariot, the son of Simon, to betray Him, Jesus, knowing that the Father had given all things into His hands, and that He had come forth from God and was going back to God, *got up from supper, and *laid aside His garments; and taking a towel, He girded Himself. Then He *poured water into the basin, and began to wash the disciples' feet and to wipe them with the towel with which He was girded.

John 13:1-5

Think about what was taking place here: Jesus *knew* Judas was going to betray Him; He knew that Peter was going to deny Him; He knew that almost down to the person all of his other disciples (except John) were going to abandon Him...and yet He got up, girded himself and washed *all* of their feet. That is what love looks like.

Love is unbounded generosity where there are needs (1 John 3:16, 17). It is taking meals together as a family (which used to be referred to as "love feasts"). Love, in a nutshell, puts others first and puts to death selfishness (Philippians 2:4-8).

Love is patient, love is kind, it is not jealous; love does not brag, it is not arrogant. It does not act disgracefully, it does not seek its own benefit; it is not provoked, does not keep an account of a wrong suffered, it does not rejoice in unrighteousness, but rejoices with the truth; it keeps every confidence, it believes all things, hopes all things, endures all things.

1 Corinthians 13:4-7

We are used to hearing this scripture in the context of a wedding/marriage, but actually, it is a charge to all of us to operate in at all times with all people. And again, the reality is that we cannot heed this charge and live it out unless we are walking in the Spirit, in grace, in mercy, and entrusting ourselves to God for the results.

"Love never fails" (1 Corinthians 13:8a).

Speaking of weddings...

The Second
Identity: Bride

Did you know that Jesus is not coming back for individual Christians (the rapture)? He is coming back for His *bride*, the church! Yes, we as individuals are a part of the bride of Christ, but Jesus is coming back for a church without a spot or wrinkle. God the Father not only wants a *family* full of sons and daughters, but He wants a bride for His Son.

> I am jealous for you with a godly jealousy. I promised you to one husband, to Christ, so that I might present you as a pure virgin to him. But I am afraid that just as Eve was deceived by the serpent's cunning, your minds may somehow be led astray from your sincere and pure devotion to Christ.
>
> 2 Corinthians 11:2, 3

"...that He might present to Himself the church in all her glory, having no spot or wrinkle or any such thing; but that she would be holy and blameless" (Ephesians 5:27).

God the Father not only wants a family full of sons and daughters, but He wants a bride for His Son.

As individuals, we are already "saints" (not sinners; Proverbs 23:7), which means "holy ones." God already sees us as holy through the blood of His Son ("justification" is the legal term for "just as if I never sinned"), and He is in the process of transforming us, which is the continuation of our sanctification from the inside-out. He has imparted righteousness (right standing) to us, and He is in the process of imputing righteousness *in* us.

Just as God wants us individually to be transformed into the image of Jesus (Romans 8:29), He desires the entire church to be corporately transformed to look like Jesus! We are called to operate in the identity of a bride that is being changed into the likeness of our Bridegroom!

"For in Him all the fullness of Deity dwells in bodily form..." (Colossians 2:9).

He (Jesus) is the *head,* and we (the bride; the church) are the *body.* Not only when the unsaved look at us as individuals should they see Jesus, but when the unsaved look at the church, they should also see Jesus. What do the unsaved see when they look at the church? Division? Pride? Self-righteousness? Judgment? Hate? Hypocrisy?

The bride's identity is about having an intimate, passionate relationship with Jesus corporately and being transformed into His likeness. As we mentioned in the foundations chapter ("Violation of Divine Design"), Jesus wants to have first place in everything.

Bae is a common modern nickname-acronym that many people ascribe to their significant others, and it means "before all else." Jesus wants to be your bae. Jesus wants to be the church's bae.

"He is also *head of the body, the church*; and He is the beginning, the firstborn from the dead, *so that He Himself will come to have first place in everything*" (Colossians 1:18; emphasis mine).

He must come before programs, plans, styles, fads, models, conferences, events, traditions...in short, everything. If we put anything before Jesus, it is, as I said in chapter three, a *violation of divine design.*

When we receive love from God the Father, we can make Jesus the center of our affection, not just as individual Christians but as the church. Sadly, I believe many churches today have fallen in love with other things: our church culture, biblical knowledge, ministry, exciting services, etc.

"Yet I hold this against you: You have forsaken the love you had at first" (Revelation 2:4).

Just like with the church at Ephesus, God wants His church to return to our "first love." The bride-to-be is in love with her Groom. Look at the Song of Songs. It is a picture of the love relationship between Jesus and His bride, the church.

The call to be the bride is a call to purity, holiness, to be sanctified (set apart) for our groom Jesus. We do this as a *body*, as well as individuals. Our corporate bodies (churches) should be examples of love, kindness, generosity, comfort, peace, goodness, and much more.

One day, hopefully soon, we will also see an end to the "church wars" over theology, doctrine, and methodology. There are too many church splits, and I pray that one day, church mergers will outnumber those churches that are getting "divorced."

The fact is, as we allow ourselves to undergo the sanctification process by the Holy Spirit, we will corporately begin to be sanctified as well.

One of the main obstacles to corporate purity these days is pride and self-righteousness. We look down our noses at the world and even other churches around us. We think we have all the right answers and that we have arrived. We preach as if we have absolute purity of doctrine. We argue, we put down, we slander, we call down fire from heaven...what a sad state of affairs!

First of all, we have no high moral ground in relation to the world. *Our* righteousness is as filthy rags (Isaiah 64:6). We were saved and delivered, not based on our deeds or worthiness, but because of His kindness, love, and mercy. Our current state is a result of God's grace and His transforming work in us.

"Such were some of you; but you were washed, but you were sanctified, but you were justified in the name of the Lord Jesus Christ and in the Spirit of our God" (1 Corinthians 6:11).

"For by grace you have been saved through faith; and this is not of yourselves, it is the gift of God" (Ephesians 2:8).

Second of all, Paul warned us not to judge those in the world: "For what business of mine is it to judge outsiders? Do you not judge those who are within the church? But those who are outside, God judges" (1 Corinthians 5:12, 13a).

Thirdly, the church down the road or across town is not your enemy. You have one enemy: the devil. The other churches in your community are not your competition.

"Who are you to judge the servant of another? To his own master he stands or falls; and he will stand, for the Lord is able to make him stand" (Romans 14:4).

This scripture applies to us equally as churches and individuals.

But maybe your problem isn't with another church per se, it's with *the church*. You were hurt, betrayed, judged, or something else happened to you that caused you to leave what you would call "organized religion."

You need the church, and the church needs you. At some point, you'll need to make a decision to leave the realm of the "walking wounded" and reenter God's designed family again.

There are no perfect churches. You and I are imperfect, and our fellowships will be imperfect. If you love Jesus, you will need to learn to love His bride.

The Bride's Purpose: Purity

We tend to focus on holiness as individuals and less as a corporate body. Sure, we preach sermons on holiness and its importance, but the sermons are usually focused on individual behavior. In order for us to pursue purity and holiness as the local church, we will need to stop focusing on our "pet peeve" sins as a Christian community and focus on the ones that keep us divided.

When we constantly preach on sin ("don't do this," "don't do that"), we are setting people up for failure and frustration. We are setting up "laws" for them that are impossible to obey simply by effort.

"For while we were in the flesh, *the sinful passions, which were aroused by the Law,* were at work in the members of our body to bear fruit for death" (Romans 7:5; emphasis mine).

When you set up "law" (legalism) in an attempt to achieve holiness, you are only strengthening your flesh.

Law only causes transgression to increase (Romans 5:20a). Example:

"I will *not* do that [sin] again!"

Your flesh: "Oh yeah? Watch me!"

Instead of considering yourself "dead to sin" (Romans 6:11), you are allowing your flesh to be aroused by establishing the law that you cannot obey (Romans 8:7).

The scriptural way to resist temptation, the flesh, and sin is by focusing on and surrendering to God instead of focusing on "not sinning."

"Submit therefore to God. Resist the devil and he will flee from you" (James 4:7).

"But I say, walk by the Spirit, and you will not carry out the desire of the flesh" (Galatians 5:16).

If we are walking in the Spirit (Galatians 5:25), focused on the things of the Spirit (Romans 8:6; Philippians 4:8; Colossians 3:1), then we will be able to resist and stand firm (Ephesians 6:13).

"What about obedience?" you may say. Yes, we are to obey His Word and His voice, but that, too, is only possible by walking in the Spirit: "...so that the requirement of the Law might be fulfilled in us, who do not walk according to the flesh but according to the Spirit" (Romans 8:4).

Remember that it is the *love* of God that motivates us, compels us to be holy.

> *For the love of Christ controls us,* having con-
> cluded this, that one died for all, therefore all
> died; and He died for all, so that they who live
> might no longer live for themselves, but for
> Him who died and rose again on their behalf.
>
> 2 Corinthians 5:14, 15 (emphasis mine)

The problem that many in the modern church have in wanting to be holy is that holiness is not an end in and of itself; it is not the goal. The goal is staying in our love relationship with Jesus, and holiness helps us accomplish *that* goal.

We don't want to be sin-focused; we want to be sin-conscious. It's the Holy Spirit's job to bring conviction and to make us holy. We want to be God-focused and love-focused (Galatians 5).

Remember that it is the *love* of God that motivates us, compels us to be holy.

What you behold, you become (2 Corinthian 3:18). Remember, you are a saint who occasionally sins, not a sinner who occasionally gets it right. We want to constantly be seeking "things above" (Colossians 3:1, 2) and keeping our eyes on Jesus (Hebrews 12:2).

Also, when you are sin-focused, you will start to see (and focus on) sin in others (Matthew 7:1-5). It's easy to find "dirt" in/on someone; God wants us to look for the gold! (See Jeremiah 15:19.) And usually, when we begin to notice sin in others, there is a good chance that we ourselves are struggling with the same thing (Matthew 7:1-5).

God calls us to be intercessors, not accusers (Revelation 12:10). Jesus is an intercessor (Hebrews 7:25), the devil is an accuser.

The call to be the bride is a call to purity, holiness, to be sanctified (set apart) for our groom Jesus. Our corporate bodies (churches) should exhibit the fruit of the Spirit just as much as we should as individuals.

When we deal with our own sin, we become more like Jesus and will be less likely to sin against others. That is a maturity process that happens within our family. We are less likely to be offended by our brothers and sisters, less likely to judge them, and by default, we will have healthier relationships, and as a result, we become more of a purified, holy bride-to-be.

When the church is walking in love and purity, we are ready to function effectively as the *body*.

The Third
Identity: Body

This, out of the five major foundational identities of the church, is probably the most presently modeled identity in our modern church culture. It has long been accepted, practiced (to varying degrees), and seen as an important part of our function as "called out ones who assemble together" (*ecclesia*, in the Greek language).

We are all, individually, members of the body of Christ, and He is the head (1 Corinthians 12). God designed the "body" in such a way that we are interdependent on one another, and we rely on each other for mutual growth and maturity.

Many Christians, however, believe and/or feel that they can be apart from the "church" (the body) and be "okay," and still mature and be used by God in a significant way. This may be true to a point or a degree, but we need to always remember: the church is God's design.

And again, the church/body is not a *building, service/ event, or organization.* It's a living organism. An eye that is unattached to its body can't see. An ear unattached to its body can't hear. A hand unattached to its body is of no use.

It is my belief that participation in an unhealthy "body," though rife with problems, is still a *better alternative* than isolation apart from the body. Both have their issues, but being in God's design is still better than being out of it.

"He who separates himself seeks his own desire and quarrels against all sound wisdom" (Proverbs 18:1).

We expect people to love us perfectly and God to disciple us. Only God loves us perfectly, and God commanded (imperfect) men/women to make disciples. Yes, we will have to navigate some messy situations, hurts, and drama, but that takes us back to the family. We must be committed to each other enough to work through the hard stuff so that we may learn to walk in unity, one with another: individually *and* corporately.

Dr. Kent Keith hit the nail on the head in his "Paradoxical Commandments":

1. People are illogical, unreasonable, and self-centered. Love them anyway.
2. If you do good, people will accuse you of selfish ulterior motives. Do good anyway.

3. If you are successful, you will win false friends and true enemies. Succeed anyway.
4. The good you do today will be forgotten tomorrow. Do good anyway.
5. Honesty and frankness make you vulnerable. Be honest and frank anyway.
6. The biggest men and women with the biggest ideas can be shot down by the smallest men and women with the smallest minds. Think big anyway.
7. People favor underdogs but follow only top dogs. Fight for a few underdogs anyway.
8. What you spend years building may be destroyed overnight. Build anyway.
9. People really need help but may attack you if you do help them. Help people anyway.
10. Give the world the best you have, and you'll get kicked in the teeth. Give the world the best you have anyway.[1]

Even though the modern American church (and that structure and culture that we've exported all over the world through missions) is flawed, the gathering of ourselves together is still essential to a healthy spiritual life, growth, and walking in the purposes of God.

Yes, the modern business model church does not allow most of the body to function in their gifts on a Sunday morning, but as we talked about earlier: "church" is not confined to Sunday mornings. We don't simply *go* to church; we *are* the church.

We don't simply go to church; we are the church.

Much of what constitutes using our gifts in the modern church model can still be defined in the light of ministry programs as opposed to true relationship. Look at the following scripture:

> And let us consider how to stimulate one another to love and good deeds, not forsaking our own assembling together, as is the habit of some, but encouraging one another; and all the more as you see the day drawing near.
> Hebrews 10:24, 25 (cf. Hebrews 3:13)

When you are isolated, you get cut off from encouragement, from comfort, from the other gifts that you need, from corporate prayer and agreement, and much more. Ultimately you cut yourself off from the "fullness of God."

"For in Him all the fullness of Deity dwells *in bodily form*" (Colossians 2:9; emphasis mine).

Jesus is the head of the church (of the body; Colossians 1:18), and we are individually members of His body. We find fullness, growth, and maturity (transformation) when we abide in Him and are a functioning part of His body. We tend to think of this in ethereal terms only sometimes when in reality, it is both a spiritual and practical matter.

Jesus lives in us through the Holy Spirit (Romans 8:9, 10); we are seated in Christ, in heavenly places (Ephesians 1 & 2); we have also been set in place in the body of Christ (Romans 12:5; 1 Corinthians 12:12; 27).

This is one-part possession and two-parts position:

1. Possession: Christ in you through the Holy Spirit (1 Corinthians 6:19).
2. Position 1: seated in heavenly places in Christ (Ephesians 2).
3. Position 2: a member of the body of Christ (1 Corinthians 12).

You need the other members of the body, *and* the other members need you! As we walk in relationship together, loving one another, serving one another, encouraging one another, sharpening one another, etc., it will lead us to be walking in the "unity of the Spirit." Remember: God desires that we would *not just* be spiritually functional but have true unity!

If we are to do these things, then one of the essential things that has to happen to us individually is we must first discover the "gifts" that God has given us. What part of the body are we? Hand? Eye? Foot?

Otherwise, what happens is that we either become "spectators" at church or we serve in an area that we may not be gifted in (*busy work* in the kingdom, where maybe there is a need, but not a match or a calling).

Have you ever taken a "spiritual gifts test" before? There are several available that are good.

How do you know what gift or gifts you have? It is one-part function and one-part grace. Do you currently operate/function in any of the gifts listed in the Scriptures? (Romans 12; 1 Corinthians 12; Ephesians 4). Do you have a "grace" for it? (Do you do it without much effort or striving?)

We also need to remember that Paul/God encourages us to "earnestly desire" (seek after) the greater gifts! (See 1 Corinthians 12:31.)

Walking in our gifts and serving others with them will require love (unconditional, selfless, and sacrificial; first foundational identity), purity (holiness; pure motives; second foundational identity), humility, and honor.

Humility is not thinking less of yourself but thinking of yourself less (Philippians 2:1-8).

Pride can not only keep us from walking in purity (holiness), but it can be a big hindrance to our walking together in unity. When we make room for others to use their gifts, we are walking in honor, as Danny Silk of Loving on Purpose defines here:

> A culture of honor is created as a community of people who learn to see others in their God-given identities. The principle of honor states that acknowledging who God says people are will position us to receive the gift of who they are in our lives and communities. In a culture of honor, leaders courageously treat people according to the names God gives them and not according to the aliases they receive from people. They treat people as friends, not slaves. As righteous, not sinners. As wealthy, not poor.[2]

In other words, honor can be seen like this: "Therefore, from now on we recognize no one according to the flesh; even though we have known Christ according to the flesh, yet now we know Him in this way no longer" (2 Corinthians 5:16).

Many churches' idea of ministry at any given service is a few leaders and a few more volunteers. This is not what we see in the early church. All were encouraged and urged to participate. Is there room at your church for everyone to use their gift(s)?

The Body's Purpose: Unity

The body was designed by God in such a way that we would need to be interdependent on one another. We would need to give to each other, serve one another, love one another in such a way that it would not only cause growth in us as individuals and the whole body, but it would result in unity.

Not conformity, but true unity in *spite* of our differences!

The first foundational trait, love, is what holds us together in unity:

"Beyond all these things put on love, which is the *perfect bond of unity*" (Colossians 3:14).

"By this all men will know that you are My disciples, if you have love for one another" (John 13:35).

And the second foundational trait, purity, is what will set us up to walk in unity: "...but if we walk in the Light as He Himself is in the Light, *we have fellowship with one another*, and the blood of Jesus His Son cleanses us from all sin" (1 John 1:7; emphasis mine).

If we are walking in love and in the light (purity), we won't have offense, unforgiveness, judgment, or sin against our brother/sister. This puts us in a prime position to walk in unity with other members of the body on all levels: local, city-church, regional and global.

One *big* obstacle that stands in the way of unity is our decision not to fellowship with other believers over our choice of doctrines and the choices of doctrines of others. Yes, while we may disagree with doctrinal positions, this should *never* keep us from fellowshipping with other Christians (assuming the doctrine is orthodox in nature and not truly heretical), and it really shouldn't prevent us from partnering with anyone for the furthering of the kingdom of God.

We should all live by this well-known creed: "In essentials [core orthodox doctrine] unity, in non-essentials liberty [freedom], and in all things charity [love]."

Agreement is important to unity (Amos 3:3), but the agreement of "what?"

This is where there is a major misunderstanding in the body of Christ. We (individuals, churches & ministries) hold tight to our own "vision" and look at other's visions and say, "I can't work with them because we don't have the same vision."

Firstly, this is why the foundation of family is important. God hates divorce. That is not just in relation to marriage. Divorce is separation. We are all in the same family, no matter what our "visions" are.

There is something *greater* than the vision that God has given you for your ministry, your church; do you know what that is? The *cause of Christ*. The Scriptures *do not* say, "Seek first the vision of your ministry..." It commands us to "seek first His Kingdom" (Matthew 6:33).

The cause of Christ and the kingdom are synonymous. Working together, partnering, encouraging, and supporting "kingdom endeavors" is something every believer, every church, and every ministry should not only be open to but should be looking for opportunities to participate in.

> **There is something *greater* than the vision that God has given you for your ministry, your church; do you know what that is? The *cause of Christ*.**

Purity opens the door for us to walk in unity, and love is what holds it together, but we must make an intentional decision to walk in unity with our other family members *despite* our diversity of vision, and yes, even diversity of doctrine (again, as long as it's orthodox).

If the focus is Jesus, then I can choose unity. If the purpose is for the kingdom, then I can choose unity. Unity (agreement) is powerful in the kingdom.

> Again, I say to you that if two of you agree on earth about anything that they may ask, it shall be done for them by My Father who is in Heaven. For where two or three have gathered together in My name, I am there in their midst.
>
> Matthew 18:19, 20

> Behold, how good and how pleasant it is for brothers to dwell together in unity! It is like the precious oil upon the head, coming down upon the beard, even Aaron's beard, coming down upon the edge of his robes. It is like the dew of Hermon coming down upon the mountains of Zion; *For there the LORD commanded the blessing*—life forever.
>
> Psalm 133 (emphasis mine)

"I [Jesus] in them and You [Father] in Me, *that they may be perfected in unity*, so that the world may know that You sent Me, and loved them, even as You have loved Me" (John 17:23; emphasis mine).

"He who separates himself, seeks his own desire; He quarrels against all sound wisdom" (Proverbs 18:1; emphasis mine).

> Therefore I, the prisoner of the Lord, implore you to walk in a manner worthy of the calling with which you have been called, with all humility and gentleness, with patience, showing tolerance for one another in love, *being diligent to preserve the unity of the Spirit* in the bond of peace. There is one body and one Spirit, just as also you were called in one hope of your calling; one Lord, one faith, one baptism, one God and Father of all who is over all and through all and in all.
>
> Ephesians 4:1-6 (emphasis mine)

The bottom line is if I am walking in the Spirit, then unity in Christ for the cause of Christ can happen. Humility is what helps us to put our "agendas" aside and work together for the greater good of the kingdom:

> Therefore, if there is any encouragement in Christ, if there is any consolation of love, if there is any fellowship of the Spirit, if any affection and compassion, make my joy complete by *being of the same mind*, maintaining

the same love, *united in spirit, intent on one purpose.* Do nothing from selfishness or empty conceit, *but with humility of mind regard one another as more important than yourselves; do not merely look out for your own personal interests, but also for the interests of others.*

Philippians 2:1-4 (emphasis mine)

This scripture doesn't merely encourage us to feign unity in some low-level ecumenicalism. Paul is pleading from the depths of his spirit for the church to put the kingdom first, to put others first.

As we discovered above, unity is very powerful in the kingdom and in the spirit realm, but it is also powerful in the natural realm (see Babel as an example; Genesis 11). The world is watching the church (universal) fight, argue, fracture, and malign each other with increasing frequency. How do we stop the infighting, come together to advance God's kingdom, and become a better witness to the world around us?

How do we stop the infighting, come together to advance God's kingdom, and become a better witness to the world around us?

I come from a very diverse family, denomination-ally speaking. We all grew up Methodist, but currently, most of my family has moved on to other choices of church association: my mom is Presbyterian; my dad is Baptist; my oldest brother is evangelical non-denomi-national, and I am a charismatic non-denominational. But you know what? We are family. Not just in the lit-eral sense, but we are a family of believers! Our church-es believe some very different things, practice some very different things, but we don't "disassociate" with each other because of those differences because we are family!

My dad's Baptist church started doing a yearly out-reach in my hometown a few years ago, during a time when my wife and I had moved back east temporarily. Christians from many different local churches came to-gether to do work projects, labors of love, service proj-ects, and acts of kindness for people and businesses in our community; no strings attached.

Nobody argued about doctrines, many unbeliev-ers in our community were blessed, and for a day, the world saw a church practically demonstrate unity and the love of God in the heart of the Bible Belt, no less.

I've been a part of several one-day events like this in our community in Southern California for many years. If we can do this for one day, then I certainly believe we can do it for the other 364 days of the year. We should *want* to do it, and we should endeavor to find or create opportunities for it to happen!

Walking in unity is what will help us transition into the next foundational identity, the *temple*.

The Fourth Identity: Temple

"You also, as living stones, are being built up as a spiritual house for a holy priesthood, to offer up spiritual sacrifices acceptable to God through Jesus Christ" (1 Peter 2:5).

As we mentioned earlier, we as individuals are "temples of the Holy Spirit" (1 Corinthians 6:19), but God also wants to "fit us together as living stones" into a "spiritual house" (Temple; corporately). When we serve one another with humility and honor, this brings us to a place of unity as His body, which invites His glory (His weighty presence).

Overview and reminder of what God required in building His temple:

1. Proverbs 24:27
2. 1 Corinthians 3:9
3. 1 Peter 2:5
4. 1 Kings 6:7

In order to get to the place of being fitted together, we will need to approach "church" differently. We must break from man-made traditions (the same things that Jesus confronted the Pharisees over) and follow the patterns we see in Scripture. We come to give, not just get.

This really is a continuation of "the body" that we just studied. You must discover your gifts and then find where you "fit" (your designed place) within the temple. We are both the priests (1 Peter 2:9) *and* the temple. When there is a unity of the Spirit, God's tangible presence and glory will begin to manifest in our midst.

As the body, we use our gifts as living stones being fitted together, which makes us the temple. As the priests, we offer our sacrifices.

"You also, as living stones, are being built up as a spiritual house for a *holy priesthood, to offer up spiritual sacrifices* acceptable to God through Jesus Christ" (1 Peter 2:5; emphasis mine).

What are "spiritual sacrifices?"

First, let me define the things I believe *are not* spiritual sacrifices, but we often think they are: many of our religious routines, especially if we've been doing them for any significant amount of time. Anything we are doing (examples: daily devotionals, going to services, volunteering at church, giving to charity, etc.) where we are "checking off our box" at the end of the day: "I've done my spiritual activity or obligation for the day and/or week!"

I'm not saying devotionals, going to services, volunteering, giving to charity, etc., are bad or that you shouldn't do them. I'm simply asking you to pose the question to yourself, "*Why* am I doing these things?" Are you doing them because you think, *This is what Christians are supposed to do?* Do you believe that by doing said activities, God will love you more or accept you more?

You must understand that there is nothing you can do to make God love you more and nothing you can do to make God love you less (Romans 8:38, 39). There is also nothing you can do (spiritual activities) that makes you more acceptable to God and nothing you can do that makes you less acceptable to God. The finished work of Jesus on the cross is the *only thing* that makes us acceptable to Him.

Remember the bronze serpent in the chapter "What is the Church?" Many times, something that God has led us into, we continue to do because it becomes habit/routine, and we keep on doing it because we've never bothered to ask God, "Is this something that you want me to continue to do?" Instead of daily following the leading of the Lord, we create a tradition.

> But in vain do they worship Me, teaching as doctrines the precepts of men. Neglecting the commandment of God, you hold to the tradition of men. [...] thus, invalidating the word of God by your tradition which you have handed down; and you do many things such as that.
>
> Mark 7:7-8, 13 (cf. Isaiah 29:13)

We often do the same thing in our churches. We do things because that is the way we've always done them. We've become comfortable in our routines and haven't bothered to check as to whether they are still giving life or producing fruit or if God still wants us to do them. Remember, God wants us to *co-labor with* Him in every area of our lives (John 5:19; Ephesians 2:10).

So, what are the spiritual sacrifices that God is looking for? God is looking for two things when it comes to sacrifice, both from individuals and the church:

1. Self-sacrifice: putting the interest of others above your own (Philippians 2:3-8), serving others (Matthew 23:11), we actually serve God *by* serving others (Acts 17:25; Philippians 2:17), dying to ourselves.

    "I appeal to you therefore, brothers, by the mercies of God, to present your bodies as a *living sac-*

rifice, holy and acceptable to God, which is your *spiritual worship*" (Romans 12:1; emphasis mine; cf. Ephesians 5:2).

Many churches create a culture that values serving in one direction: people are there to serve the church and its vision. And while there is an element of that which is right and true, serving should always go both ways; and in fact, it is incumbent upon those in leadership to model it at a higher level (see the Matthew 23:11 verse above; cf. Luke 22:24-27; John 13:12-17).

2. Sacrifice of praise (worship): just as the priests in the Old Testament were in charge of the offerings at the Temple, we are to offer sacrifices to God, both individually and corporately.

   "Through Him then, *let's continually offer up a sacrifice of praise to God,* that is, the fruit of lips praising His name" (Hebrews 13:15; emphasis mine).

Prayer should be highly valued in our gatherings; after all, one of the identities of the church is a "house of prayer" (Matthew 21:13a). Worship (celebration, praise, and adoration), too, should be highly valued.

But many of our church cultures give prayer only a few minutes out of our allotted time together, and the time of worshipping (singing) is often looked at as preparation for the sermon. As someone who has been on staff as both a pastor and a worship leader in several churches, I can tell you that a good percentage of the congregation look at the worship time as optional, just based on their arrival times after the service has started.

The word "worship" has its origin in the compound word "worth-ship," which means "that which you give the highest value to." And yes, we can use it in a very broad sense to mean that we value God above all else, but in this specific case, let's look at it within the context of musical worship, of which the Scriptures give us a plethora of examples.

David discovered the importance of worship and the manifest presence of God as an individual long before it became widely available to everyone else. His prayers, psalms, and songs made it clear that it was what sustained him.

"One thing I have asked from the Lord, that I shall seek: That I may dwell in the house of the Lord all the days of my life, to behold the beauty of the Lord And to meditate in His temple" (Psalm 27:4).

O God, You are my God; I shall seek You earnestly; My soul thirsts for You, my flesh yearns for You, In a dry and weary land where there is no water. Thus, I have seen You in the sanctuary, to see Your power and Your glory. Because Your lovingkindness is better than life, my lips will praise You. So, I will bless You as long as I live; I will lift up my hands in Your name. My soul is satisfied as with marrow and fatness, and my mouth offers praises with joyful lips.

Psalm 63:1-5

David began to experience this revelation of the nearness of God through his worship. Here he was the youngest son, sent out to watch sheep with only a sling and a harp while his brothers went off to war. He was so overlooked by his own family, he wasn't even invited to his own coronation.

But through his worship, he found a place where he belonged.

He discovered a place of contentment (Psalm 23:1), a place of rest and restoration (v. 2-3), a place of protection (v. 4), a place of provision and overflow (v. 5), and a place of acceptance and unconditional love (v. 6).

David was so moved by these worship-God encounters personally that when he became the king, he desired that the rest of the nation of Israel be able to have the same experience. He set his heart on recovering the Ark of the Covenant (which represented the presence of

God), establishing 24/7 worship at the Tabernacle, and building God a temple.

David's worship encounters were so anointed and powerful that they even drove off demons!

> Now the Spirit of the Lord had departed from Saul, and an evil spirit from the Lord torment-ed him. [...] One of the servants answered, "I have seen a son of Jesse of Bethlehem who knows how to play the lyre. He is a brave man and a warrior. He speaks well and is a fine-looking man. And *the Lord is with him.*" [...] Whenever the spirit from God came on Saul, David would take up his lyre and play. Then relief would come to Saul; he would feel bet-ter, *and the evil spirit would leave him.*
>
> 1 Samuel 16:14, 18, 23 (emphasis mine)

This is the kind of worship that we should desire, both individually and corporately: where God's pres-ence is manifest, and it changes us as individuals, and it changes the atmosphere around us. We will discuss this in greater detail in the final foundational identity.

The Temple's Purpose: Glory

There are two types of glory found in the Scriptures, so I'd like to define them for you: "glory" (*doxa* in the Greek language) means "thoughts, opinions, and recognition."

This is the glory spoken of in a very familiar passage in Romans 6:23: "...for all have sinned and fall short of the glory of God."

The Greek word for "sin" in this passage is an archer's term, and it means "to miss the mark." What is the mark (bullseye)? We have all sinned and fallen short of God's thoughts, opinions, and recognition of who we are called/purposed to be (Psalm 139:16).

Glory (*kavod* in the Hebrew language) means "weight, heaviness, majesty."

When God's presence would manifest tangibly in the Bible, it was so heavy and weighty it often would render people helpless or unable to move (2 Chronicles

5:13, 14). King Saul was so overcome by the Spirit of God that he had these experiences:

> As Saul turned to leave Samuel, God changed Saul's heart, and all these signs were fulfilled that day. When he and his servant arrived at Gibeah, a procession of prophets met him; the Spirit of God came powerfully upon him, and he joined in their prophesying. When all those who had formerly known him saw him prophesying with the prophets, they asked each other, "What is this that has happened to the son of Kish? Is Saul also among the prophets?"
>
> So, Saul went to Naioth at Ramah. But the Spirit of God came even on him, and he walked along prophesying until he came to Naioth. He stripped off his garments, and he too prophesied in Samuel's presence. He lay naked all that day and all that night. This is why people say, "Is Saul also among the prophets?"
>
> 1 Samuel 10:9-11; 19:23, 24

And this was before the promise of Joel:

> "And it shall be in the last days," God says,
> "That I *will pour out My Spirit on all mankind*;
> And your sons and your daughters will proph-
> esy, and your young men will see visions, and
> your old men will have dreams."
>
> Acts 2:17 (emphasis mine; cf. Joel 2:28, 29)

For our study here, we will focus on the Hebrew word for "glory" and its definition.

God's promise of His Spirit was not only to be in us (1 Corinthians 6:17, 19) but to be on us (with us) as well (John 14:17). Throughout the ministry of Jesus and the first church in the book of Acts, we see the saints experiencing powerful encounters of God's manifest presence or a move of His Spirit.

Unity in the Spirit brings the tangible presence. When both Old Testament and New Testament saints were unified, they experienced powerful times of the manifest presence of God:

> When the priests came forth from the holy place (for all the priests who were present had sanctified themselves, without regard to divisions), and all the Levitical singers, Asaph, Heman, Jeduthun, and their sons and kinsmen, clothed in fine linen, with cymbals, harps and lyres, standing east of the altar, and

with them one hundred and twenty priests blowing trumpets in unison when the trumpeters and the singers were *to make themselves heard with one voice to praise and to glorify the Lord,* and when they lifted up their voice accompanied by trumpets and cymbals and instruments of music, and when they praised the Lord saying,

"He indeed is good for His lovingkindness is everlasting," *then the house, the house of the Lord, was filled with a cloud, so that the priests could not stand to minister because of the cloud, for the glory of the Lord filled the house of God.*

2 Chronicles 5:11-14 (emphasis mine)

When the day of Pentecost came, they were all together in one place. Suddenly a sound like the blowing of a violent wind came from heaven and filled the whole house where they were sitting. They saw what seemed to be tongues of fire that separated and came to rest on each of them. All of them were filled with the Holy Spirit and began to speak in other tongues as the Spirit enabled them.

Acts 2:1-4 (unity; cf. v.44)

If you are a believer and have been for any amount of time, you have most likely experienced His tangible presence. You might have been alone in a time of prayer or worship, or you may have been in a corporate setting.

Let me share one of my experiences. As I mentioned before, I grew up in a Methodist church. When I became a Christian at the age of seventeen, I set out to find a more energetic and lively church, which I found two towns over. It had modern worship, and I experienced the tangible presence of God and moves of the Spirit there with regularity.

One day in the middle of worship, I heard an inner voice telling me that I needed to go back to my Methodist church. I rebuked that voice saying, "Get thee behind me, Satan!" But then God spoke up and said, "That wasn't the devil, it was Me!" I asked God, "Why would you make me go back there after experiencing such life here at this church?"

God replied, "I'm sending you back because I'm about to send a Spirit-filled preacher there. He will need your support." Sure enough, a month later, Pastor Joe was appointed to the Methodist church I grew up in. Pastor Joe was there for four years before moving on, and I could tell you of many amazing testimonies of how God moved among us during that time. I'll share one specific testimony.

One Sunday morning, as the service was starting, God decided to show up in a very tangible way. Nothing seemed out of the ordinary as the choir walked down the aisle towards the choir loft in the front of the sanctuary, singing "To God be the Glory" by Fanny Crosby out of the hymnal. It seemed with each verse and chorus, the intensity grew and the congregation sang with greater fervor.

You literally could sense the moment that it felt like God stepped into the sanctuary. Heavy, weighty presence.

When we reached the final verse and chorus, the organist and the piano player stopped playing, and the tall, vaulted cathedral ceiling was reverberating with raucous a cappella singing! When the song ended (and nobody wanted it to end), there was silence for a good five minutes as *everybody* was soberly aware that the presence of God was among us in a tangible way.

Pastor Joe, after allowing the congregation to soak it in, eventually prayed us into the rest of our service, and I still get goosebumps when thinking about that moment, even now while writing.

I found this out later after having several conversations with people in our church about that Sunday morning, but what I thought was just savvy musicianship was anything but. When the piano player and organist dropped out musically towards the end of the song, it was because the presence of God had so over-whelmed them that they were weeping and could no longer play!

God wants moments like that to be normal like they were in the Bible and not rare.

"Yet You are holy, You who are enthroned upon the praises of Israel" (Psalm 22:3). Another translation says, "You inhabit the praises of Your people" (KJV).

As my friend and worship leader Rick Pino says, "Our worship should build a throne for God to inhabit."

It's not about having certain feelings or emotional-ism; it's about what happens when God reveals Himself to us in such a way that we cannot deny it and we dare not resist it.

Things that can happen when God's glory (tangible presence) is manifest:

1. Conviction and Salvation (Acts 2)
2. Revelation of God's character (Moses; Exodus 33, 34; Psalm 16:11)
3. Gifts are imparted (Acts 10)
4. Transformation (2 Corinthians 3:18)
5. Healing (Luke 5:17)
6. Sanctification (Exodus 29:43)
7. God's kingdom is established ("His rule & reign"; Matthew 6:10)

His glory among us changes us, challenges us, and encourages us to walk in boldness, the way the early church did.

His glory among us changes us, challenges us, and encourages us to walk in boldness, the way the early church did. It helps us understand that God is powerful and nothing is too difficult for Him (Jeremiah 32:27). It puts us in a prime position to see God move on our behalf and even fight for us:

> "Listen, all you of Judah and the inhabitants of Jerusalem, and King Jehoshaphat: This is what the Lord says to you: *'Do not fear or be dismayed because of this great multitude, for the battle is not yours but God's.* Tomorrow, go down against them. Behold, they will come up by the ascent of Ziz, and you will find them at the end of the valley in front of the wilderness of Jeruel. You need not fight in this battle; take your position, stand and watch the salvation of the Lord in your behalf, Judah and Jerusalem.' Do not fear or be dismayed; tomorrow, go out to face them, for the Lord is with you." Jehoshaphat bowed his head with his face to the ground, and *all Judah and the inhabitants of Jerusalem fell down before the Lord*, worshiping

the Lord. The Levites, from the sons of the Ko-hathites and from the sons of the Korahites, *stood up to praise the Lord God of Israel, with a very loud voice.*

They rose early in the morning and went out to the wilderness of Tekoa; and when they went out, Jehoshaphat stood and said, "Listen to me, Judah and inhabitants of Jerusalem: Put your trust in the Lord your God and you will endure. Put your trust in His prophets, and succeed." *When he had consulted with the people, he appointed those who sang to the Lord and those who praised Him in holy attire, as they went out before the army and said, "Give thanks to the Lord, for His faithfulness is everlasting." When they began singing and praising, the Lord set ambushes against the sons of Ammon, Moab, and Mount Seir, who had come against Judah; so, they were struck down.* For the sons of Ammon and Moab rose up against the inhabitants of Mount Seir, completely destroying them; and when they had finished with the inhabitants of Seir, they helped to destroy one another.

2 Chronicles 20:15-23 (emphasis mine)

The Fifth Identity: Army

We have progressed from the foundational "loving family" to His "pure bride" to the "unified body" to the "temple full of His glory," which puts us in a position to walk in the final major foundational identity of the church: His powerful *army*.

Paul refers to us being soldiers enlisted in God's army in 2 Timothy 2:1-4 and mentions the armor of God (Ephesians 6) and spiritual warfare (2 Corinthians 10), but it's the Old Testament where we see many examples of the army of Israel literally fighting battles where many of our spiritual warfare principles come from.

Many in the modern church want to disregard the Old Testament; some not outright, but they will say things like, "Since we are not under law [Mosaic Covenant], we only adhere to New Testament principles."

But in the New Testament, we find these gems:

"For whatever was written in earlier times was written for our instruction" (Romans 15:4a).

"Now these things happened to them as an example, and they were written for our instruction" (1 Corinthians 10:11).

Yes, we are no longer "under the law" in the sense that we can obtain righteousness by observing the law, although I don't think that was ever the case. Abraham's example, Hebrews, chapter eleven, in general, and a few New Testament scriptures show us that it has always been "faith" that has pleased God and been the instrument/requirement by which we obtain righteousness.

So, why all the animosity towards the Old Testament?

Jesus said in Matthew 13:52, "Therefore every scribe who has become a disciple of the kingdom of heaven is like a head of a household, who brings out of his *treasure things new and old*" (emphasis mine; cf. Matthew 5:17).

There is a faulty viewpoint and erroneous theology being propagated by some folks in various Christian and church circles that minimize the Old Testament, ignore the Jewishness of the Scriptures and the early church, and say Israel has no future prophetic significance.

Yet, the Old Testament is more than just "stories that have morals": it is full of timeless truth and powerful principles equally as potent as anything in the New Testament:

"The sum of Your word is truth, and every one of Your righteous ordinances is everlasting" Psalm 119:160 (emphasis mine).

We as individual believers and as the army of God need all of the weapons we can get: "In the word of truth, in the power of God; by the weapons of righteousness for the right hand and the left" (2 Corinthians 6:7).

In the Old Testament, we see how God ordered His army and had the different tribes trained in different ways so that they could attack the enemy in different ways: King Jehoshaphat and David's mighty men whose exploits were legendary; Elisha and his servant and the army of God that surrounded the enemy's army (2 Kings 6:17).

Yet, of course, we know that our battle is not in the physical realm, against people, but against the devil and his demons. Imagine what we could do if the church would stop fighting each other and actually go to war united together against our only real enemy!

> For our struggle is not against flesh and blood, but against the rulers, against the powers, against the world forces of this darkness, against the spiritual forces of wickedness in the heavenly places.
>
> Ephesians 6:12

**Imagine what we could do if the
church would stop fighting each other
and actually go to war united together
against our only real enemy!**

There is a *big* difference between being an individual soldier in God's army and walking as the army. Soldiers don't win battles or wars by themselves; armies do. Yes, we are called to put on our armor and carry our sword (Ephesians 6:10-17). Yes, "the weapons of our warfare [...] are divinely powerful for the destruction of [strongholds]" (2 Corinthians 10:3-5). Yes, God has given us authority as believers (Luke 10:19, 20), *but* it is tied to the "earthly realm."

"The heavens are the heavens of the Lord, but the earth He has given to the sons of men" (Psalm 115:16).

We have authority as individuals to heal the sick, to bind and loose, cast out demons, etc., but God has not given us authority as individuals to displace "rulers and principalities" in the heavenly (spirit) realm. This is a far bigger teaching than I have the room or time for here, but suffice it to say, this is where many Christians get into trouble while engaging in this type of spiritual warfare.

First, they go at it alone, and that opens them up to all kinds of pushback from the enemy, and secondly, they have not walked in the progressive identities of the church that allow for God to bring victory in the bigger spiritual battles that we may face. For a deeper understanding of these principles, I recommend the late John Paul Jackson's book *Needless Casualties of War*.

God wants the church to engage in spiritual warfare as His army so that He can bring victory about on our behalf.

"So that the manifold wisdom of God might now be made known *through the church to the rulers and the authorities in the heavenly places*" (Ephesians 3:10; emphasis mine).

For a surefire *individual* spiritual warfare strategy, I recommend the following:

"Good overcomes evil" (Romans 12:21). "Light overcomes darkness" (Romans 13:12; Ephesians 5:8, 13; 1 Thessalonians 5:5). If you want to shut the gates of hell, open the windows of heaven.

Do good. Be light. Love well. Pray. Forgive. Bless. Be generous. Serve. These things do much more damage to the kingdom of darkness than we realize.

We are not to be ignorant of the devil's schemes (2 Corinthians 2:11), but we shouldn't focus too much on the enemy, just as we mentioned we shouldn't be too focused on sin/not sinning. The only One worthy of our constant attention is our God.

Behold, I have given you authority to tread on serpents and scorpions, and over all the power of the enemy, and nothing will injure you. Nevertheless, do not rejoice in this, that the spirits are subject to you, but rejoice that your names are recorded in heaven.

Luke 10:19, 20

Jesus is saying to His guys, "Hey, that's great that you cast out some demons, but let's get our focus back where it belongs...on the kingdom!"

By all means, put on your armor and take up your sword (Ephesians 6:10-17); use truth in your arsenal to tear down strongholds (2 Corinthians 10:3-5). But please do it in the context of the Spirit-led army of God (the church). Be prayerful and make sure you have heard the Lord clearly before engaging our spiritual enemy.

As I mentioned at the end of the last chapter, God wants to fight for you. Did you know that our *worship is warfare*?

There is an important connection between being the temple (where worship is the primary activity) and being the army (where warfare is the primary activity). These two identities work together in a major way. We looked at how King Jehoshaphat ordered the worshippers out ahead of the army in 2 Chronicles, chapter twenty. When the praises of God went up, God brought the hammer down, so to speak! This is not an isolated incident. We have several scriptures that point to the truth that when we worship God, He wars on our behalf.

Now, given a choice, would you rather:

A) Engage in spiritual warfare against the enemy by yourself and deal with all of the ramifications of those battles, or

B) worship God and let Him fight the enemy for you?

Let's look at some examples of this in the Bible:

Sing to the Lord a new song, sing His praise from the end of the earth! You who go down to the sea, and all that is in it; you islands, and those who live on them. Let the wilderness and its cities raise their voices, the settlements which Kedar inhabits. *Let the inhabitants of Sela sing aloud, let them shout for joy from the tops of the mountains. Let them give glory to the Lord and declare His praise in the coastlands. The Lord will go out like a warrior, He will stir His zeal like a man of war. He will shout; indeed, He will raise a war cry. He will prevail against His enemies.*

Isaiah 42:10-13 (emphasis mine;
cf. Psalm 98:1; Psalm 27:5, 6)

Behold, the name of the Lord comes from a remote place; His anger is burning and dense with smoke; His lips are filled with indignation, and His tongue is like a consuming fire; His breath is like an overflowing river, which reaches to the neck, to shake the nations back and forth in a sieve, and to put in the jaws of the peoples the bridle which leads astray. *You will have songs as in the night when you keep the festival, and gladness of heart as when one marches to the sound of the flute*, to go to the mountain of the Lord, to the Rock of Israel.

And the Lord will cause His voice of authority to be heard, and the descending of His arm to be seen in fierce anger, and in the flame of a consuming fire in cloudburst, downpour, and hailstones. *For at the voice of the Lord Assyria will be terrified, when He strikes with the rod. And every blow of the rod of punishment, which the Lord will lay on him, will be with the music of tambourines and lyres; And in battles, brandishing weapons, He will fight them.*

Isaiah 30:27-32 (emphasis mine)

Praise the Lord! Sing a new song to the Lord, and His praise in the congregation of the

godly ones. Israel shall be joyful in his Maker;
The sons of Zion shall rejoice in their King.
They shall praise His name with dancing;
They shall sing praises to Him with tambou-
rine and lyre. For the Lord takes pleasure
in His people; He will glorify the lowly with
salvation. The godly ones shall be jubilant in
glory; They shall sing for joy on their beds.
*The high praises of God shall be in their mouths,
and a two-edged sword in their hands,*
To execute vengeance on the nations, and pun-
ishment on the peoples, to bind their kings with
chains, and their dignitaries with shackles of iron,
to execute against them the judgment written.
This is an honor for all His godly ones. Praise
the Lord!

Psalm 149 (emphasis mine)

Then on the seventh day they got up early at
the dawning of the day and marched around
the city in the same way seven times; only on
that day did they march around the city sev-
en times. And at the seventh time, when the
priests blew the trumpets, Joshua said to the
people, "Shout! For the Lord has given you the
city." So, the people shouted, and the priests
blew the trumpets; and when the people

heard the sound of the trumpet, the people shouted with a great shout, and the wall fell down flat, so that the people went up into the city, everyone straight ahead, and they took the city.

Joshua 6:15-16, 20

In the story of Gideon, God defeated the armies of Midian with a dream, 300 men, pitchers, torches, and trumpets (Judges 6:15-22). We've also looked at the Old Testament examples of King Jehoshaphat and Jericho, where God fought on behalf of His people. But you might be asking, "Where do we see this in the New Testament?"

Now about midnight Paul and Silas were praying and singing hymns of praise to God, and the prisoners were listening to them; and suddenly there was a great earthquake, so that the foundations of the prison were shaken; and *immediately all the doors were opened, and everyone's chains were unfastened.*

Acts 16:25, 26 (emphasis mine)

God also supernaturally delivered Peter from prison through the prayers of the saints (Acts 12).

"For the eyes of the Lord roam throughout the earth, so that He may strongly support those whose heart is completely His" (2 Chronicles 16:9a).

"'Teacher, which is the great commandment in the Law?' And He said to him, 'You shall love the Lord your God with all your heart, and with all your soul, and with all your mind'" (Matthew 22:36, 37).

One of the ways that we demonstrate our love towards God (in response to His love; 1 John 4:19) is to worship Him with all of our heart. When we do that, He strongly supports us. When the church engages in corporate prayer and worship, God shows up to strongly support us and fight on our behalf.

The Army's Purpose: Power

"For the kingdom of God is not in words, but in power" (1 Corinthians 4:20).

Well, there it is. God wants to move in power. In us, on us, through us and in our midst, and through us as a corporate body.

Most people generally like things neat, tidy, clean... but warfare is messy. Power is often messy.

"Where no oxen are, the manger is clean, but much increase comes by the strength of the ox" (Proverbs 14:4).

The ox in this Scripture represents power. When there are no oxen, there is no poop. Sure, you can have less drama and mess in your church because you are afraid of what might happen if people start moving in power, but trust me, your mess will still be there (in other areas), and you will see little change in your neighborhoods, your city, and even your congregation.

Powerless Christians and churches exist in every city. They may have good music, they may present good teachings, they may have friendly, loving people, but they are changing little in the spiritual atmosphere and usually changing very little in their communities.

God calls us to forcefully (in the spirit realm) advance His kingdom here on the earth (Matthew 11:12). He calls us to push the darkness back and to even plunder Hades itself (Matthew 16:18b).

Whether this happens through unified corporate prayer (James 5:16b; Matthew 18:19) or through people being allowed to exercise their spiritual gifts (1 Corinthians 14) or taking the gospel to the streets, with signs and wonders following (Romans 15:19), this is what we are called to as the church.

God has promised us that the same Spirit that raised Jesus from the dead works within us. Yes, He wants to make you holy, but He also wants to move in power, in you, and through you.

God's desire is to transform us into the image of His Son (Romans 8:29), and Jesus came to destroy the works of the devil (1 John 3:8), and that not only includes sin, it includes sickness, strongholds, bondages, and anything else demonic.

You know of Jesus of Nazareth, how *God anointed Him with the Holy Spirit and with pow-*

er, and how He went about doing good and healing
all who were oppressed by the devil, for God was
with Him.

Acts 10:38 (emphasis mine)

There is no neutral ground in the spiritual realm, no demilitarized zone. We will either be taking ground or losing ground to the enemy. This applies to us as individuals, as well as the church.

Jesus promised that the gates of Hades would not prevail against (overpower) the church (Matthew 16:18). The last time I checked, "gates" were not an offensive force; they are a defensive structure. The church is supposed to be taking ground from the enemy offensively.

There is no neutral ground in the spiritual realm, no demilitarized zone. We will either be taking ground or losing ground to the enemy. This applies to us as individuals, as well as the church.

How does the church accomplish this? By walking in power and authority collectively.

And the congregation of those who believed were
of one heart and soul; and not one of them

claimed that anything belonging to him was his own, but *all things were common property to them. And with great power the apostles were giving testimony to the resurrection of the Lord Jesus,* and abundant grace was upon them all.

Acts 4:32, 33 (emphasis mine)

The early church is our model here. They walked in love, purity, unity, regularly experienced God's glory (manifest presence), and operated in the power of the Holy Spirit. They saw the blind see, the deaf hear, the lame walk, and the dead raised. If that was God's heart, desire, and will for people back in the time of Jesus and the early church, why would it be any different today?

"Jesus Christ is the same yesterday and today, and forever" (Hebrews 13:8).

The short and most scriptural answer is: it isn't. God is still in the business of miracles, healing, signs, wonders, and gifts of the Spirit. To Him, the supernatural is natural. It's what He does because it's who He is.

"While You extend Your hand to heal, and signs and wonders take place through the name of Your holy servant Jesus" (Acts 4:30).

"Therefore, they spent a long time there speaking boldly with reliance upon the Lord, who was testifying to the word of His grace, granting that signs and wonders be performed by their hands" (Acts 14:3).

"All the people kept silent, and they were listening to Barnabas and Paul as they were relating all the signs and wonders that God had done through them among the Gentiles" (Acts 15:12).

"In the power of signs and wonders, in the power of the Spirit; so that from Jerusalem and all around as far as Illyricum I have fully preached the gospel of Christ" (Romans 15:19).

Yes, the Gospel has the *power* to bring salvation (Romans 1:16), and the Holy Spirit works powerfully within us to transform us (Colossians 1:29; Romans 8:29), but God also wants to work powerfully *through us* to change the world *around us*!

We have been given authority in the name of Jesus, and we have the power of the Holy Spirit within us *and on us*. If we want to see the results of the early church (salvations, deliverances, healings, etc.), we must walk in the things they walked in (1 Corinthians 11:1; 1 John 2:6; 4:17).

God also wants to work powerfully through us to change the world around us!

If we want to establish God's rule and reign (His kingdom; Matthew 6:10) in our communities and cities, the church will need to do battle together. The local church and the city church must walk in love and purity towards each other and in unity for the cause of Christ, above all other agendas.

When we begin to do this, we will start to experience His glory and walk in His power, and we will see major victories in the spiritual realm.

In Conclusion

As I've said before, most of us in the modern Americanized Church culture have devolved into the idea that the church is a *building, a service/event, or an organization,* or a combination of the three. The nation of Israel and the Jewish people ended up at the time of Jesus in this same dilemma. Their relationship with God had devolved in a similar fashion.

By the time Jesus strolled onto the scene, the Jewish people's relationship with God was a *building* (Temple), an *event/service* (the Sabbath), and an *organization* (the priesthood).

The purpose of God for the whole nation of Israel was that it was to be a light to the nations (Isaiah 42:9; 49:6). Where did they get off track? Where did they trade a relationship with God for "form and function"?

In Exodus, chapters nineteen and twenty, God declared His desire for Israel to be a "kingdom of priests and a holy nation." All throughout the Book of Exodus (19:5; 23:21, 22) and really through the entire Old Testament, we see over and over again the command to "obey His voice." Even in verse eight of chapter nineteen, the children of Israel agreed with God: "All that the LORD has spoken we will do!"

A little further on at Mount Sinai, God had told Moses to keep the people from going up the mountain or touching it, lest they die. Here's where things get interesting:

> Then they said to Moses, "Speak to us yourself and we will listen; but do not have God speak to us, or we will die!" However, Moses said to the people, "Do not be afraid; for God has come in order to test you, and in order that the fear of Him may remain with you, so that you will not sin." So, the people stood at a distance, while Moses approached the thick darkness where God was.
>
> Exodus 20:19, 20

God didn't say, "If I speak to them, they will die." He only warned them not to come up to or touch the mountain. This reminds me of Eve in the garden in Genesis, chapter three. God said, "Don't eat of the fruit of the tree of knowledge." But she relayed to the serpent, "We are not to touch the fruit, or we will die." This is exchanging the truth of God for a lie (Romans 1:25).

And shortly after this, Israel was worshipping the "creature instead of the Creator," the golden calf.

This major shift for Israel, where they went from obeying God's voice to not wanting to hear directly from God for themselves, put them in in a place where they eventually as a people missed their time of visitation, when God Himself, Jesus the Messiah, was standing in front of them (Luke 19:44).

We must see the church and be the church that God designed. We must see the church as a living organism that we are a vital part of and the others in the body are vital to us. We must come to give and not just get. We must return to the age-old foundations and build according to God's divine design. We must be willing to exchange our old wineskins for new wineskins.

We must see the church and be the church that God designed.

We must walk in the five major foundational biblical identities of the church: God wants *sons*, not servants (family); God wants *laid down lovers* (bride); God wants *ministers*, not members (body); God wants a *nation of priests* (temple); God wants *worshipping warriors* (army).

I cannot stress how important it is that you, as a collective body of believers, start at *the foundational identity*: the family! As I mentioned in the chapter "The Purposes and Corresponding Traits," each identity builds on the prior one. As we learn how to operate in each prior identity, it molds us, prepares us, and empowers us to be successful in the next identity. Being a family and learning how to love is the most important starting point to being the church God desires!

Thank you for taking the time to read this book. I pray that the Lord used many things in the context of this book to bless you, sharpen you, challenge you, and encourage you.

Stay tuned for a follow-up book on the church coming soon!

Notes

1 Kent M. Keith, *The Silent Revolution: Dynamic Leadership in the Student Council* (Cambridge, Massachusetts: Harvard Student Agencies, 1968), 18.

2 Danny Silk, "What Does Honor Look Like? Fruit to Look For in the Culture You Are Creating around You," Loving On Purpose, September 26, 2016, https://lovingonpurpose.Com/Blog/What-Does-Honor-Look-Like/.

About the Author

Doug is currently a co-senior leader, along with his wife Monica, of Our Refuge LA in Southern California. Our Refuge is a network of house churches, with a mother church in Virginia and a sister church in Atlanta. Originally from Radford, VA, Doug has lived in the Los Angeles area since 1998.

Doug has been married to his wife Monica since 1993. They have both been in full-time ministry through the length of their marriage. Together they have taught Cleansing Stream for a number of years, have been trained in Wellspring Ministry, and have trained hundreds in ministry training and deep ministry. They also co-wrote a twelve-week discipleship training curriculum called the Foundation Manuals.

Doug helped Rick Sizemore, the senior leader of Our Refuge Churches, start Eagle's Nest Campus Ministry at Radford University in 1991. Doug & Monica did a one-year internship with Rick ministering on the campus of Radford University and Virginia Tech and took over the campus ministry at Radford University the following year. They continued ministering to students until 1998 when they felt led to move to Southern California.

Doug is also a worship leader who has led worship and been a speaker at youth events, college campus ministry events, and many different churches over the years. He is currently working on writing various books during this season from his experiences during thirty-five years of full-time ministry.

If you'd like more information or have questions, please feel free to contact Doug at:

5foundationsbook@gmail.com.